Hi Jerry,

Best wishes

Brian

Praise for Brian Smith and
The Birth of a Brand

As an entrepreneur myself, I found this book to be an eye-opener for me and very likely for most entrepreneurs. For me, there was one *aha* after another that will help me plan and execute future business strategies. Thank you, Brian for your business insights!"

—**Dr. Tony Alessandra**, hall-of-fame keynote speaker and author, *The New Art of Managing People* and *The Platinum Rule*

"What a ride! This book is a case study of lessons learned from failure. Read, reflect, and implement strategies that will help you achieve business success. The underlying current of providing incredibly good customer service is critical for any business wanting to stand the test of time. Good on ya, Brian!"

—**Tom Hopkins**, author, *How to Master the Art of Selling*

"As a successful entrepreneur, Brian doesn't 'own the t-shirt,' he's got the boots to prove it. You'll learn much about business and life as you follow his interesting journey to build a major brand."

—**Mark Sanborn**, author, *The Fred Factor* and *You Don't Need a Title to be a Leader*

"Success is a journey, and I encourage you to read Brian Smith's *The Birth of a Brand*. As a very successful entrepreneur, this book relates the story of how learning to face obstacles can lead to success that most people only dream about."

—**Don M. Green**, executive director, Napoleon Hill Foundation

"Wow! An exciting, captivating life adventure of ups, downs, and twists that will stir your spirit, stimulate your creative imagination, and light your fire! It's a valuable read that will re-kindle your emotions, germinate new ideas, and revitalize your life!"

—**Ed Foreman**, entrepreneur, US Congressman (Rtd.), Texas and New Mexico

"A captivating and compelling read! This book shares the story of the grit and determination that it takes to build a massively successful business! Brian Smith teaches lessons that not only help you to grow your business, but also to grow yourself. Read it and reread it— I highly recommend this book!"

—**Dr. Willie Jolley**, CSP, CPAE, Speaker Hall of Fame member, author, *A Setback Is a Setup for a Comeback* and *An Attitude of Excellence!*

"Brian Smith brings to life the journey every entrepreneur faces in making his dream a reality. *The Birth of a Brand* will give you perspective and encouragement to get through the tough days and a foretaste of the satisfaction you'll feel in overcoming obstacles and achieving success. Best of all, you'll find real-life insights and practical tips you can use in making your dream take flight. Don't just buy this book; live it."

—**Terry Paulson, PhD**, national columnist, speaker, and author, *The Optimism Advantage*

"*The Birth of a Brand* is vintage Kipling, when he wrote, 'To meet with triumph and disaster and treat those two imposters just the same.' You will enjoy Brian's trek because in it you will find the essence of your life's journey."

— **Dr. Jim Tunney**, educator, author, and former NFL referee

"Brian Smith's *The Birth of a Brand* is a must-read for every college business major for its wisdom and insight into launching a billion-dollar business. Written in a highly engaging style, Brian's message will resonate with the entrepreneurial you as you join him on his seventeen-year journey to capture the hearts and feet of America. Incredible lessons of courage, determination, and creating opportunities can be practically applied to any business that strives for success. You cannot put this book down until you've read it through, highlighted every principle, and begun putting them to work in your own business."

—**Hank Boyer**, CEO, Boyer Management Group

"*The Birth of a Brand* provides the reader with tremendous insight into business and life. As you read about Brian's journey, it becomes clear that he is not only a gifted storyteller and successful entrepreneur, but a keen observer and student of business and the critical variables that make it work. This is a great read for anyone interested in the real factors that make a business successful!"

—**Mitch Fairrais**, president, The Learning Experience Company, Inc.

"Success is not a theory. It is a follow-the-leader proposition. This book is required reading for all entrepreneurs, especially those struggling in the 'infancy stage,' where most people give up. Brian's description of the seven stages of the business life cycle will illuminate the way you think about your business forever."

—**Jim Stovall**, bestselling author, *The Ultimate Gift*

"A compelling story full of valuable takeaways any business person can use. It is a feel-good book where the numerous trials are overcome by super triumphs. Startup entrepreneurs need to put this tremendous book on their must-read-soon list."

—**Patrick O'Dooley**, CSP, author *Flight Plan for Living*

"Need a boost? Brian Smith spent more than a decade dealing with adversity without giving up. And he succeeded! If he did it, you can too! This book will give you straight talk and inspiration. Read it!"

—**Vicki Hitzges**, international motivational speaker and enthusiastic UGG wearer

"Brian's book reads like a mystery novel—with intrigue, antagonists, tragedy, and celebration—but it's a real story with real people in a real company. And Brian gives us many strategic insights from what he learned along the way. Highly recommended reading."

—**Stephen Tweed**, CSP, CEO, Leading Home Care

"*The Birth of a Brand* will energize the entrepreneurial mind. Brian demonstrates how courage and determination can withstand any adversity one might face on their journey to success."

—**Dr. Joe L. Dudley, Sr.**, co-founder, Dudley Products, author, *Walking By Faith*

The Birth of a Brand

Launching Your Entrepreneurial Passion and Soul

Brian Smith

BEYOND WORDS

20827 N.W. Cornell Road, Suite 500
Hillsboro, Oregon 97124-9808
503-531-8700 / 503-531-8773 fax
www.beyondword.com

Beyond Words Publishing is an imprint of Simon & Schuster, Inc., and the Beyond Words logo is a registered trademark of Beyond Words Publishing, Inc.

For more information about special discounts for bulk purchases, please contact Beyond Words Special Sales at 503-531-8700 or specialsales@beyondword.com.

Manufactured in the United States of America

10 9 8 7 6 5 4 3 2

Library of Congress Cataloging-in-Publication Data

Smith, Brian, 1946-
    The birth of a brand : launching your entrepreneurial passion and soul / Brian Smith.
        pages   cm
        1. Smith, Brian, 1946-   2. Businessmen--Australia—Biography.   3. Footwear industry.
    4. Product management.   I. Title.
    HC602.5.S59A3   2014
    338.7'68531092—dc23
    [B]
                                                                                            2014022874

ISBN 978-1-58270-535-4
ISBN 978-1-58270-537-8 (eBook)

The corporate mission of Beyond Words Publishing, Inc.: *Inspire to Integrity*

Contents

Preface

I don't recall learning to surf. It just happened. Around the time I was seven or eight, I would borrow one of the immense, hollow wooden surfboards belonging to the local surf lifesavers club and play for hours in the two-foot-deep whitewater, dragging the board out from the beach and balancing on it as the swells made it rise and slide, and then pushing off on small waves that carried me a few seconds to the shore.

Before long, I was seeking out bigger waves, eventually those twelve- or fifteen-foot-high monsters that made it feel like I was jumping from the top of a building, savoring the long moments of free fall as the board teetered on the crest and dropped into the face.

My passion for surf has driven me to this day, affecting where I have lived, worked, and vacationed for more than forty years. Surfing, like sailing, becomes a way of life, allowing you to see the world from the shoulder of a vastly more powerful presence than yourself. It sets human endeavor in proportion and reminds you that setting a goal and reaching it is never solely the result of your own effort; it's a negotiated partnership with the universe.

My favorite surf of all time is still ingrained in my senses as if it just happened. A summer sunset at Broulee Beach—I was in my late teens. The warm air and water embraced me, and the surf was almost flat with only an occasional one-foot swell rolling below me. For more than an hour, I sat on my board, looking inland toward the setting sun, mesmerized by the orange sky and the millions of ripples stirred by the offshore wind. Every time a wave rose to break, a spray of luminous red, gold, and purple droplets blew skyward. Around dark, I paddled the short distance to shore.

It was the only time in my life that I've had a surf without catching a single wave.

It was the closest I've come to touching the hand of God.

To this day, whenever I make it "out the back," behind the breaking waves, I offer a little prayer of gratitude—for that experience, for that partnership with the universe. It can give me goose bumps just thinking about it.

• • •

That connection with the universe—it has always guided me. When I moved to America, it guided me. When I started UGG, it guided me. There have even been times when it saved my life.

In 1978, I was twenty-eight years old, single, and after an unfulfilling career as a chartered accountant, I had no idea what I wanted to do with my life. The late-afternoon sun was shining through the window of my living room where I sat amidst the discarded wrapping of my new Pink Floyd album *Dark Side of the Moon*. Setting needle to groove, I had no idea that my world was about to change. The song "Time" began, describing the drifting way many of us live our lives and how our youth leads us to believe that we can put things off indefinitely, and I heard the lyrics, "No one told you when to run / You missed the starting gun." The power of those words reached into my soul.

I sat bolt upright, and my body became covered in goose bumps (my higher self's way of letting me know I am on the right track). I thought of all my accounting friends who were working toward the coveted partnerships and others who were running successful businesses, and realized I had been running in place for ten years. I'd missed the starting gun. I had a strong voice inside me telling me that the life I was living was not in harmony with what I really wanted.

I had recently bought a book on Hatha yoga and was practicing the basic poses. What struck me about yoga was its ability to get me out of my head—out of my body even—and into a different level of awareness. It had helped me inadvertently discover meditation.

During one of these sessions, my mind was relaxed, remote from the dissonance around me, and it kept drifting off into random thoughts about businesses and consumer products. It occurred to me how many of the cool products that fit the lifestyles of my Australian buddies—Levi's jeans, water beds, skateboards, surf clothing brands—had come from the United States. Suddenly, my whole body erupted with goose bumps again. As clear as a bell, I heard the call to go to America, find the next big hit lifestyle product, bring it back to Australia, and build my own business around it—and I listened.

Less than six weeks later, my friend Margot, who I had met just a few years earlier when she was vacationing in Western Australia, met me at the Greyhound station in L.A. My oversized plastic yellow suitcase strapped to the back of her MG Midget, we headed to her apartment in the hills above Hollywood—and I headed, full speed, into my new life.

JAG Jeans, the company that Margot worked for, had sent her to L.A. to help open an American office. JAG was the hottest clothing brand in Australia, and they hoped to duplicate that success in the United States. Margot introduced me to her friends, who would change the direction of my life. Doug Jensen, her former boyfriend, was a surfer who introduced me to the delights of surfing Malibu. He had already made friends with two Aussies, Brett Livingston-Strong and his brother Paul, who were living in a car at the time and were in L.A. to display about five tons of sculptures and artwork they had transported from Australia.

Margot set me up with a job in the warehouse at JAG, and on weekends, we all made the drive to Moorpark in Simi Valley to a big grassy hill where we took turns sliding down it on Brett's newfound contraption, grass skis. These consisted of U-shaped aluminum frames under which several wheels were attached in a curve so that, when their wearer leaned to put weight on their edges, the wheels followed an arc, simulating snow ski turns.

I was a sucker for Brett's enthusiasm for grass skiing's potential, and I was totally convinced this would be the next big thing, a world-changing new sport. I had found what I was looking for! I knew I needed to go back home, sell a small rental property I owned, and use the cash to finance my new venture.

Since my destiny was in fact to be played out in America, and sheepskin boots would indeed prove to be my mainstay, I now know this was the universe's "carrot on the stick" to draw me from Australia. I am a firm believer that when you take those first baby steps, you don't have to know exactly where you are going to end up. If you do not take the first steps, then you will never come across the forks in the road that lead to new opportunities for growth.

I flew home, my house sold immediately, and I returned to L.A. Within a day of getting off the plane, I had found a place within a fenced-in area in Venice that had three tiny one-bedroom homes renting for two hundred bucks a month. Margot and Doug knew L.A.'s neighborhoods better than I did, and when I told them how finding something so cheap must be a sign of my karma at work, they tried to talk me out of signing the lease, to no avail. I was in no mood for naysaying . . . though I did notice that every house on the street had bars on the windows.

I bought a water bed and kitchen utensils, wall hangings, and a twelve-inch-tall candle I placed on the shelf that ran around the living room. I treated myself to a solitary house-warming party my first night. I bought a pizza and a bottle of wine, pulled out the rack of tapes from my suitcase, and turned the boom box up. I lit the candle (without bothering to put a dish under it), poured myself some wine, and lay back to contemplate my future as a tycoon in the grass-skiing industry.

I woke up around nine the next morning with a groggy awareness that my new home was not as it should be. When I sat up, everything went black and I found myself gagging, struggling for breath. I crouched back down; my mind went into full alert. I looked toward the living room and realized it was filled with black smoke that hovered about a foot above the main floor level.

Shiiiiiit! The house is on fire!

I rolled out of bed and crawled on my stomach to the front door. Off to the right, a purple-orange radiance was pulsing behind the smoke. I knew I only had minutes to get out. Taking a big breath, I reached up and tried to open the door . . . and found it was stuck. Seeing flames flickering above me, I fumbled at the latch repeatedly but had to keep dropping to the floor to take in air. My mind was racing. If the front door was out of the question, how else could I escape? Every window in the house had bars bolted to the outside. The only route to the back door led through the worst of the flames.

I had a vivid awareness of my body relaxing as I slumped to the floor, and said out loud, "F***. I'm going to die."

Now, you might find what I'm about to tell you a bit difficult to accept—but I heard a voice. It wasn't a voice that came through my eardrums. I knew it was not my usual internal monologue, but something very different: a clear, calm, unhurried voice that said: "You have not done enough with your life yet, Brian."

Damnnn! You're right!

I felt a surge of energy, jumped to my feet, and felt my way along the wall. Window by window, I started punching out the glass with my fist, screaming, "Help!" through the openings and then ducking down to the floor for more air before rising up to scream for help again.

I worked my way along the wall until I got back to the sunken bedroom with its life-saving air pocket, and punched out the last window, still screaming for help. The air pocket gradually became unbreathable, and I was forced to push my face out through the glass shards, my forehead pressed against the steel bars, and gasp for air as the smoke poured over my shoulders, into the clear, sunny day outside.

Then I heard voices yelling, "Hang on, we're almost there!"

A construction worker who had been remodeling a house down the street set about using his crowbar to pry the bars off the window; every few seconds, he had to retreat to get fresh air. The bars came off one-by-one, and after an eternity, strong hands pulled my shoulders through the opening as I heard approaching sirens.

I came to on the steps of a neighboring house, coughing violently and retching up chunks of ash.

• • •

I have a few thoughts about the significance of that voice that saved my life. This was not the first time I had experienced a supernatural life-saving event. Twice before I had sensed a strange intervention that kept me safe.

Call it God or guardian angels or whatever you will, I am convinced there is some sort of intelligence that speaks to all of us on this planet but we do not yet fully understand how to tune in. While we're all looking for a God that is somewhere far off in the heavens, that Presence is here within us, guarding us and keeping us safe.

I also wonder if this spark of intelligence has a definite plan for our time on earth, if we would only listen to it on a daily basis instead of having it only come through in times of despair or desperation. Maybe the great men and women of history had this ability.

What I know is, that day I was out past the break, I came the closest to this Presence I've ever been, but there are moments in my life when I feel it near me again—when it reveals itself to me in one way or another. And I listen to that voice and let it guide me. I've learned that not only does that spark of intelligence help me when I'm in danger, but it also guides me in business. It sometimes seems that the world of business is filled with Gordon Geckos and conmen, but if you mentally paddle out the back, rest calmly on the water, and just watch the spray of the waves, you can tune in to the voice that will help you deal with these types and figure out how to creatively move forward and become wildly successful—while also living a fulfilling, authentic life.

Introduction

This is partially my story and partially the story of a product—a simple product, practical, comfortable, and in its own way, peculiarly elegant—with an unlikely brand name that millions of consumers have come to value and trust.

It now has worldwide recognition, but it began when I was a novice businessman, a disenchanted chartered accountant and terrified salesman, who put my trust in pure instinct, goose-bump shivers of recognition that I was in the presence of a sure thing, faith that the universe supplies whatever's needed, and the reassurance of a quiet, mysterious inner voice those many times when accounting figures said the venture was hopeless.

Is there such a thing as a born entrepreneur? Possibly. I've met a few who qualify. But I hesitate to claim to be one myself. I only know that I was open and ready when the universe put the object of my inspiration into my hands.

And that's the other part of this story: the story of how I was (and still am) and how you can be open to the universe in business—how you can be creative and successful while also being true to yourself.

What I know for certain is that each of us is born with a creative nature. But ours is an evolutionary planet and nothing, from a flea to an oak tree to an ocean-going liner, comes into existence fully formed.

One thing I've realized: You can't give birth to adults.

I am the proud parent of two beautiful daughters as well as the founder of a successful brand. For my fellow entrepreneurs just starting out, I can attest that the stages of the two ventures are amazingly similar.

It doesn't matter whether the product is a new shoe, a new device, a new religion, or a new sitcom, every new paradigm follows the same growth curve:

- **Conception:** There is the blissful aha, then, little by little, the concept continues to take embryonic shape.
- **Birth:** The concept is introduced to the world and attracts the first true believers who love it with all their heart.
- **Infancy:** The concept just lies there, needing lots of feeding and constant attention.
- **Toddler years:** It begins to crawl, then stands up and reaches out, and you don't dare take your eyes off it for an instant.
- **Youth:** The passing of weeks and months falls into a routine that is more or less predictable and enjoyable. Healthy growth seems natural and surprisingly controllable, yet every time you turn around there are unexpected expenses and needs. You struggle to keep up.
- **Teens:** They seek popularity and want to be at all the parties, everywhere at once, setting the world on fire. Rules are broken, and despite your best efforts at establishing controls, they refuse to be contained.
- **Adulthood:** With luck and hard work, the child survives in the real world. Expectations become realistic and growth settles into a manageable long-term pattern. The product begins paying for itself! Basically, it can now stand on its own at last; however, sometimes, real opportunities are overlooked or discounted as mature judgment overrules unbridled enthusiasm.

Building a business—just like raising children—takes work and determination. That's not news. Over the course of the first seventeen years of building the UGG brand and observing other businesses, I noticed some common themes: great expectations on pitiful budgets, unshakeable optimism, and grinding endurance in the face of unforeseen setbacks. I have no doubt these have been the defining characteristics of entrepreneurs since time began.

They're also the essential characteristics of every proud parent.

In This Book

What follows is my own story, and the story of UGG.* I break down each year, the cash flow, the major setbacks as well as the major successes, the ever-changing structure of the company, and the moments when the universe spoke to me in the form of aha moments, goose bumps, or even a strong intuition of dread.

Along with my story, there are sidebars throughout that explain the ins and outs of business—key terms, financial explanations, and general rundowns of retail. For anyone interested in learning more about business, unfamiliar with a term, or just curious about retail, hopefully you'll find these elements helpful.

Here and there, you'll also see what I call Wisdom Points throughout that further illuminate a philosophy that I learned at that time or that simply crystallized at that time, and that have helped me not only in business but also personally. These are also inspired by the many business books and authors I've read over the years, as well as wisdom from the mentors I've been lucky enough to have come to know along the way. One thing I've realized is that who you are in business is who you are in life, and when you act with integrity, stay true to your ethics, and just treat everyone with simple respect, you'll be successful, but more importantly, you'll be happy.

---

* Author's Note: This book spans the first seventeen years of building the UGG brand. Beginning with the first early adopters on the beaches of California, I slowly expanded into the ski areas and eventually established UGG as a casual comfort brand across America. After the sale of my company to Deckers Outdoor Corporation in 1995, I remained an interested observer, but played no part in the ongoing management of the company. Full credit for the success of UGG growing into a billion dollar global lifestyle brand goes to Connie Rishwain, President of UGG and the Deckers team led by Angel Martinez, President and CEO.

• • •

It would be nice to believe that you can throw a business plan, staff, cash, and projections into a pot, assemble enough lawyers and MBAs in a conference room to watch, and launch a successful brand fully formed. But nine women can't have a baby in a month, right?

It doesn't work that way. Building brand awareness is a slow, often disheartening process requiring imagination, constant monitoring and feedback, course corrections, persistence, and above all, patience. The success of any concept requires bringing whole markets and wide swaths of a society around to a new vision. Building a brand, like any natural process, is a gradual, organic, and wildly unpredictable experience.

And building your own philosophy as you work is something that will happen as you build your brand—whether you want it to or not. So, to the fledgling entrepreneurs reading this story: Welcome and best wishes! Buckle up. It's a going to be an interesting ride.

CHAPTER 1

CONCEPTION AND BIRTH

"She'll be right, mate!"
1979—Sales $1,000

Without exception, from the moment you have your "aha" moment as an entrepreneur, it becomes enshrined in your memory forever. It may take a long journey of preparation to arrive at that moment of conception, to be ready to recognize and receive it, but the gestation that follows is equally necessary. Many factors might have to come into alignment before those first actions of giving birth. Such things can't be rushed, and in the meantime, life goes on.

Goose bumps had started rising on the backs of my hands and forearms, spreading up over my shoulders, and shivering down my back.

In my hands was the latest issue of *Surfer* magazine, open to an advertisement showing two sets of legs in front of a cozy fireplace, with the feet clad in sheepskin boots. Everything about the ad was absurdly out of place in a magazine published in Southern California and devoted to surfing, palm trees, girls in bikinis, beaches, bare legs, bare feet . . .

But the ad screamed at me, "You're going to be a huge success!" I'd been in California less than six months, and here was my future staring back at me from the pages of *Surfer*.

My surfing and grass-skiing buddy Doug Jensen was in the room when my revelation hit. I showed him the picture.

"I don't get it," he said. "Boots? Who wears boots?"

"Exactly," I said. And nobody did! Not in America—but in Australia, where sheep outnumber people, it seemed like half the population owned some sort of sheepskin footwear, and certainly no surfer would be caught dead without at least one pair of sheepskin boots.

But there were no sheepskin boots in America.

If half of all Americans—or even half of one percent of all Americans—bought sheepskin boots, and I was the only one selling them . . . *My God. I'd be rich!*

The voice inside me had been right all along. The problem was that I had gotten its message backward! My destiny wasn't to come to America, find the next big thing, and bring it back to Australia. The next big thing was already in Australia. My destiny was to bring it to America, where I would be wildly and immediately successful.

> *A vision of big success is typical of the blind optimism shared by most people during the "aha" moment when they conceive their new dream. I believe that for a true entrepreneur, some degree of ignorance is a key ingredient for success. If you knew at the time all the obstacles you're up against, you'd never even start.*

In my case, I was totally ignorant of the fact that Americans had little knowledge of the amazing attributes of sheepskin being rugged, breathable, washable, and above all, comfortable. To them it was hot, sweaty, prickly, delicate, and good for jackets and mittens—not footwear.

For Australians, sheep are such a central fact of life that it's near impossible to get through the day without some kind of dependence on them. If

I had realized this culture clash at the outset, I probably would have tossed the magazine aside and gone back to dreaming of skiing the grassy hillsides of Australia.

Instead, my first step was to contact the company that had placed the ad in *Surfer*, Country Leather in Western Australia, to get some sort of exclusive agreement to sell their products in the United States.

I called immediately and spoke with Country Leather's owner, George Burcher.

"I've had a lot of calls from the United States from people wanting to distribute our boots," he told me.

"Well, let me tell you why you should pick me," I began, realizing I would have to make him as convinced as I was that I was the right guy. I told him that, like him, I was a West Aussie, from Perth, and that I was an accountant looking to start my own business. I told him I'd raced in the National Windrush Surf Cat sailing championships in his hometown, Albany, and I recounted every other piece of Aussie trivia I could think of to try and create a bond between us.

He said he'd get back to me after he did some checking.

I found out much later that he called the Department of Trade in Perth, where he was connected with a guy named Jim Nylander, who just happened to be a good friend of mine from the Soaks rugby club. Jim gave me a big thumbs-up for trustworthiness and assured George I was smart enough to handle the importing of boots.

The universe had kicked in, and though I didn't need to listen this time, I'm grateful George did.

Armed with a go-ahead from Country Leather, Doug and I agreed to partner up and test the market in Southern California. Since Doug had no fear of selling, we decided that he would be the salesman and I would handle the back-office business.

The first obstacle we faced was that we were both broke. In order to get started, we needed samples to show prospective customers. We pooled our fortunes and came up with five hundred dollars. I sent Country Leather an order for six pairs, three for Doug and three for me, in various sizes, to be shipped by airmail.

Ours was very typical of the beginning of most distribution arrangements. Most often through travel, one might find an item from one area that is missing back home and samples are bought to take back and test the market to see if consumers will buy. Christopher Columbus brought tobacco back from his travels. Phil Knight tested samples of running shoes from Asia on his way to branding Nike. Usually, if the tests prove positive, then a more formal distribution agreement is formed between the buyer and seller, and they both endeavor to build the volume of sales, helping each other out.

We called the styles Short, Medium, and Tall, and Natural was the only color. Doug set out on the road to begin visiting shoe stores in Southern California.

On the brand-building end, I immediately decided that "country" and "leather" had to go, along with the image of ski-lodge fireplaces. Warm, cozy settings implied slippers, but I envisioned these boots being worn in outdoor environments.

I knew from my time in Sydney that local surfer and businessman Shane Stedman had registered the name UGH for sheepskin boots in Australia, yet I could find no evidence that any of the boots had been marketed or sold in the United States under that name. I began the process for registering a trademark, UGG, for our business venture.

A week or so later, Doug came back from his road trips feeling pretty down. No one in the shoe trade really got what the boots were about. They wondered why on earth we were trying to sell sheepskin in Southern California. Didn't we know it never got cold here? So far, we had no orders.

A footwear trade show was coming up in New York, so, armed with our three pairs of Short, Medium, and Tall boots and nothing else, I set out to conquer the national footwear industry.

New York is not the city to be in when you have no money. I checked into a cheap hotel near the convention center. Walking the streets I was scared, with images of muggings, murders, and rapes in the park in my head, so I was on full alert. On the way to the convention center, I kept a death grip on my small bag of samples, in case a snatcher tried to separate me from my life's new purpose.

All I could afford was half a display space, and since I had registered as an exhibitor at the last minute, I found my "half-table" located in the back of the hall, near the end of the aisle next to the toilets. I had no money to rent backdrop drapes or a carpet to cover the bare concrete floor. I had no logo, no photos, and no brochures, only a crude, photocopied price list for the multitudes of buyers I expected to be ecstatic that somebody had finally brought sheepskin boots to America.

If those goose bumps while reading *Surfer* signaled the moment of conception of the sheepskin-boot venture and the act of purchasing samples from Australia its birth, then Doug's road trips and the New York trade show were the beginning of a very long and trying infancy. For three days, only those buyers who happened to be lost or on their way to the bathroom walked by my table. I followed their eyes as they looked at the four-dollar espadrilles from Spain on my left, skipped over my display as if it were an empty space, and then refocused on the cheap pumps from Taiwan on my right. I might as well have been displaying fresh fish or auto parts. The table received zero glances, zero questions, not even a flicker of perplexity or curiosity. Nothing.

Each evening I walked back to my hotel room dejected, but each morning I was filled with fresh enthusiasm that indeed that day would be the day.

Three days was a long time to endure indifference to our three pairs of boots. As I packed up to go home, I found myself searching my soul for direction: Should I give up? Was this too hard? Why the hell didn't Americans get sheepskin?

By the time I got on the plane back to Santa Monica, I had mapped out the next steps we needed to take. My dormant marketing neurons were beginning to fire.

At the show, two things had become clear. First, no one had a clue about the benefits of sheepskin boots. Second, no one even recognized sheepskin boots as a category within the US footwear industry.

"But in Australia, every other person seems to own some sort of sheepskin footwear," I kept saying to myself. I owned a pair, and I knew how good they were. These same reassuring thoughts would save me many times over the next five years, whenever things looked too damn hard and I contemplated ditching the whole idea.

As I mulled things over, it occurred to me that my California friends to whom I'd shown the samples from Australia were mostly surfers, and they invariably told me about their friends who had made the surfing pilgrimage Down Under and brought back five or six pairs of boots, for themselves and for their buddies back home. They recounted what I already knew: When you get back to the beach after an hour or two in cold water, the best feeling in the world is a pair of sheepskin boots, wet feet and all. The wicking nature of the fleece evaporates the moisture, and the insulating properties immediately bring warmth back to your feet. These were two vitally important pieces of product knowledge lost on the New York buyers—and on Americans in general.

I discussed this with Doug, and we decided to refocus our efforts on surf shops. He would handle the San Fernando Valley, and I would cover the beach stores.

• • •

I procrastinated. I was terrified! I was an accountant whose closest contact with the subculture of salesmen had been during my stint as an auditor at a used car lot in Perth, and to me they had seemed like an alien species. The courage required to cold-call strangers and try to sell them something was a huge emotional stretch for me.

Days stretched into a week. Driven by the guilt that Doug was already on the road, I realized I could procrastinate no longer. I opened the yellow pages and made a list of all the surf shops in Malibu, Santa Monica, Manhattan Beach, Hermosa Beach, and Long Beach, all the way down to San Diego, and one sunny morning in September, I drove my white Dodge van to Con Surfboards, the first store on my list. Timidly pulling my boots out of my dilapidated Adidas bag, I asked to see the owner.

When he saw the shoes, he said, "Wow, sheepskin boots! I have a pair my friend brought back from Oz on his last trip. Those are great!" We talked surfing for a while, and his final words as I left the shop were, "If you're going to import those boots, you're gonna make a killing."

Wow, this is the validation I was hoping for, I thought as I climbed into my van and looked up the route to the next stop. At each shop, I had a similar reception: "My friends have some of these, and they love them." E.T. Surf in Manhattan Beach, Dewey Weber Surfboards, Becker's Surf and Sport in Hermosa Beach, Newport Surf & Sport, Jack's Surfboards in Huntington Beach, Laguna Surf and Sport—every owner said the same thing.

Meanwhile, Doug was getting a similar reaction in the Valley at Val Surf and the Glen Kennedy Surf Shop. The next day, I set out for San Diego. By now I felt bulletproof—that is, until I got to South Coast Surf Shop in Ocean Beach. When I pulled out my samples, the owner, Rob Ard, just burst out laughing.

"Hey, Jim," he called out to his surfboard shaper in the back of the shop. "Come out here! Some Aussie is trying to sell sheepskin boots to a surf shop!" Jim worked his way through the racks of clothing, took one look at the boots, and cracked up. I was mortified. All of my fears about selling flooded back. I wanted to be invisible.

"Just kidding," Rob said once he noticed the look of terror in my eyes. "Those boots are great. A ton of guys we know have some. It's about time someone started selling them in the States. That's a killer product. You'll do well with them."

As horrific as that felt, Rob did me a big favor. I realized that my fear in this case had been unfounded, and after this, I was able to differentiate between the product being rejected, versus me being rejected. It took some time, but eventually I would walk into any store committed to connecting with the buyer on human terms first, before showing the product I was selling.

Driving home that afternoon up Interstate 5, it never occurred to me that I had not asked for a single order. A minor detail. I didn't know you had to! What was the point? We had no inventory to ship, and anyway, I was so carried away with how successful we were going to be that booking actual orders was just a minor detail. Soon I would learn that one of the most enduring truths taught in all sales training courses:

Nothing happens until there's a sale.

•   •   •

The next weekend, Doug and I were comparing our experiences from our surf shop campaign, asking each other how we were going to get the product we needed, and we came to the only conclusion we could come to: we had to raise some money.

My roommate, Dorsey Roach, overheard one of our discussions and offered to introduce us to some investors. Dorsey had been hired by Exxon six months earlier. His job was to buy oil rights in the Los Angeles area. He had befriended a family who had inherited a substantial number of leases they were now selling to Exxon, and they were looking for alternative investments. Dorsey arranged a meeting where I met Mack and Angie Rhodes and their sons, Steve and Jeff. Mack was a motorcycle cop for the LAPD. Steve and Jeff were in their early twenties and eager to find business opportunities. Since this was my first time raising capital, I was fully optimistic. I described the level of interest we had just encountered in the surf shops and explained how popular sheepskin boots were in Australia. It was no doubt evident we didn't have a very sophisticated business plan. Nonetheless, our enthusiasm generated an offer from the Rhodeses to back us with a $20,000 investment.

A week later, we met with them at their attorney's offices in Newport Beach. I had previously been doing business as a sole proprietorship, so we decided to create a formal legal partnership. We set up the new company as UGG Imports and went 50/50 with the Rhodes family.

While we were waiting in the lobby of the law firm, discussing our great future, I noticed a magazine on the receptionist's desk: *Action Sports Retailer*, volume one number one.

I borrowed the magazine and scanned it, and realized it was the first issue of a trade magazine targeted specifically to the owners of surf shops and sporting goods stores in the heretofore unnamed "action-sports industry." There it was—our platform for making our new product known to the surf market. I was experiencing a phenomenon I'd later find described in self-realization books:

Once you set a new course and take action, the universe will conspire to work with you.

I'm sure everyone has seen this concept discussed in one way or another, whether it's called manifestation *or* prayer, *or just starting on your path while being open to the signs that the universe will send you. It's been an important part of how I do business, and it's always worked: when I've begun a venture that I truly felt was my destined path, things fell into place and people came into my life to help it happen.*

Stated another way, you never notice advertisements for refrigerators unless you decide to buy a refrigerator. Then you see ads everywhere. The signs are always there, but only when you start on your path do you take notice.

I asked the receptionist where she got it, and she told me friends of hers were the founders and they were looking for advertisers.

We signed the legal documents that formalized our partnership, and Mack Rhodes handed me a check for $20,000. We were made! We would never need more seed money again! We were on our track to instant success.

Had I been aware that I needed to think through a five-year business plan, taking account of salaries, traveling and warehouse expenses, marketing, advertising and trade shows, staffing and shipping costs, cash flow forecasts to warn of the horrific problems of a seasonal business not to mention thin profit margins, and so on, I would have realized that I needed a half-million dollars or more to have a fighting chance of survival. But the flip side is that if I knew that, I might have simply walked away thinking it was too hard, and the UGG brand might not exist in the market as it does today.

Nowadays, I highly recommend entrepreneurs know what the road ahead of them looks like. There are several excellent business plan software programs available that will walk you effortlessly through the thinking process for starting out on your new venture.

We called George Burcher at Country Leather in Australia and told him of our money-raising success, and that we wanted to buy inventory. Immediately we encountered an ugly reality.

Since you never know what size feet are coming into a retail store, you have to be ready with sizes five through twelve, which amounts to eight pairs. But sizes seven, eight, and nine are the most common, so you need to stock more of those than the others. *But* since men have bigger feet than women, you also need a good ratio of nines, tens, elevens, and so on. We began to see that every store had to have a minimum of fifteen pairs of a style to ensure *one* customer could be satisfied.

We quickly realized that because we wanted to "open up" many retail stores with boots, we were going to have to carry a huge inventory in order to supply them with their original orders and fill-ins for when they ran out of sizes ("open up" means opening up shelf and display space within each store.)

We ordered about five hundred pairs of assorted sizes, in the three styles and two colors; then I went to the bank and wired $15,000 to George.

A quintessential hippie, George grew up in the far south region of Western Australia, as did his wife, Helen. Starting out selling small, hand-worked leather goods and trinkets at swap meets and farmers' markets, they eventually became store owners on the main street of Albany, catering to the summer tourists. They also opened a small sheepskin products factory with a single sewing machine to do the leatherwork. Bit by bit, they developed the sheepskin boot business, to the point where Country Leather was among the biggest employers in the area. George was a fit and passionate rider of waveskis, a cross between a surfboard and a kayak. His infectious smile and bald head made him stand out among the town's colorful characters.

Right from the beginning, my intuition was clear that George and I were destined to clash. I was aware of the immense size of the American market and knew it would take many manufacturers to supply it, so I was going to build the business with that eventuality in mind. George, on the other hand, believed *he* was building the American market, with me as his salesman.

Everyone views their surroundings from their position at the center of their own universe. Lots of universes can coexist as long as they are in alignment with an overall design (a common purpose), but when two are on a collision course, the resulting convergence will cause a complete realignment of one if not both universes. Clashing universes are the norm, whether it is between a mother and child, husband and wife, boss and coworkers, or the leaders of nations.

George promised he would airfreight our boots within the month, so we began learning about customs brokers, sales price lists, and size charts. I went to the stationery store to buy order pads and blank invoice forms for all those sales we were going to make.

Doug Jensen and I drove to South Laguna to meet with the owners of *Action Sports Retailer* magazine. Jeff Wetmore and his wife, Suzie, were the editorial and production team, and Steve Lewis was the ad salesman. They had a small office just off Pacific Coast Highway, looking toward hills dotted with beach houses and trees.

I could see from their expressions that cozy sheepskin boots were not the kind of thing they were expecting to advertise in an action-sports magazine. On the other hand, they were beginning to close the materials for their second issue, and as a good salesman, Steve knew that any sale was better than nothing. He zeroed in on the sale smoothly, making it clear a full-page ad normally went for $1,100 but—simply because he liked us and our product—if we would commit for two months, we could get in for only $1,000 each.

"No way," I told him. "We haven't even shipped product yet, and we're way too small to be running full-page ads."

Without missing a beat, Steve came back with a marketing tip that would serve me well for years to come:

"It's not how big you are that matters," he said, "but how big you're perceived to be."

Perception is extremely important in life, because the majority of people accept what they see as reality. Whether it is clothes and grooming in face-to-face meetings, the style of car you want to be seen in, or the image your product or service portrays, people judge you on your first impression. In the case of UGG, ever since Steve gave me that advice, I went out of my way to make sure the image we presented in advertisements, trade show booth decorations, brochures, and packaging was as good as we could make it.

Nowadays, however, with the internet commanding such a widespread influence, the website has become the face of the company, product, or service, but the principles of advertising and promotion have not changed. Perversely, the internet has completely leveled the playing field since a new vendor operating out of a garage can look every bit as expensive and professional as an established business. I advise all new entrepreneurs to put every effort into making their website look like a million dollars, as the perception of viewers from all over the world is what counts. They will not likely come to your garage to verify your size.

Looking at Doug, I had no doubt what he wanted. We signed a two-month contract.

Now all we had to do was invent a marketing concept that would define our brand for years to come, put together an impressive and professional-looking full-page magazine ad, and have it camera ready within days, all on a marketing budget of essentially zero. Doug's former wife was an artist, so we recruited her to create the artwork and copy for the ad.

Doug brought it by when it was finished. My heart sank. I expected a photo of the boots and some cool graphics and descriptions of the product. Instead, here was a long-haired hippie dude with his robe flowing in the wind, holding a globe of the world. The art was due the next day though, so we went with it.

For the next issue's ad, we retained the hippie dude, only this time he was gazing at a crystal ball displaying a vision of sheepskin boots.

Three weeks later, seventeen cartons cleared customs and were being held at a bonded warehouse near Los Angeles airport. We juggled the cartons into our truck, and back at my house in Santa Monica, we cleared out the third bedroom, now officially "the warehouse," and stacked it full of boxes.

When we opened the first box, an alarm went off in my head. We opened the second box and the alarm grew louder. After six boxes, I knew we were in trouble.

The boots had thin, micro-cell rubber soles that were glued to the bottom of the sheepskin uppers. Whoever had done the gluing apparently hadn't been taught to keep the glue off the soft leather. It probably hadn't been very noticeable when the glue was still wet, but as it dried, it turned brown. Ugly brown smears were plainly visible on almost half of the boots in the shipment.

But that wasn't the worst problem.

In some pairs, the left boot was constructed of soft leather but the right boot was made of a different, stiffer skin. When you set them side by side, one boot stood up by itself the way it was supposed to, while the other collapsed, looking despondent.

Half the shipment seemed to have been constructed from skins with short, curly fleece a quarter of an inch long. The other half had long, straight fleece about three quarters of an inch long. Some pairs had one boot with the curly fleece while the other had straight.

There's a saying in Australia that's not quite as famous as "shrimp on the barbie." Whenever all hell breaks loose, a proper Aussie gives a wink and says, "She'll be right, mate!"

So there we were, late in the afternoon in our new warehouse, pondering how we were going to mate-up pairs of odd and dispirited-looking boots that even the least discerning American consumers would buy.

I called George. "Oh, she'll be right, mate," he told me. "Just sell 'em like they are. That's what we do down here."

Naturally. My mind flashed back to the first sheepskin boots I'd bought years earlier at the Hay Street flea market, mixing and matching my own pair from odd-lot boxes, and I realized how right George was. Australian consumers were accustomed to putting up with a degree of challenge, finishing the work the manufacturer had begun themselves. We thrive on it; it suits our self-reliant, adventurous spirit. That was just the way sheepskin boots were back then, rough hewn and individualized. It would be twenty years before the requirements of a global market filtered back to Australia and a handful of manufacturers evolved products—through a feedback loop of incremental improvements—with enough consistent quality to satisfy the standards of American consumers.

With the van full of boots, I once again set out for the beach to visit Con Surfboards.

I opened my order book, and said, "Okay, how many do you want?"

"Oh, Brian, I know these are great, and you're going to make a killing, but we couldn't sell them out of this shop. Our customers just want surf shorts and boards. We hardly even sell sandals. But good luck! You're gonna do great!"

And so began the longest three days of my life, driving from one surf shop to the next, pulling out samples and the order book, being told the same thing over and over: "We can't sell them out of our shop . . . They're too expensive for our customers . . . We love them but . . . You ought to try the shoe stores."

On day three, Doug and I convened in the "warehouse" to write up our orders.

Surfboards by Kennedy, 5 pairs:	$174
California Foam Co., 8 pairs:	$284
Howard Furman (a friend), 1 pair:	$30
Val Surf, 7 pairs:	$268
E.T. Surfboards, 7 pairs:	$244
TOTAL: 28 pairs:	$1,000 even!

We stood back and stared up at the stacks of shipping boxes rising to the ceiling.

I thought, *Ohhhh shit!*

Clockwise from top left: Brian surfing Broulee Beach, Australia.
Top right: Original UGG boot sample Brian brought to the United States.
Bottom right: Deposit slip of the first year's sales.
Bottom left: First UGG advertisement in *Action Sports Retailer*.

CHAPTER 2

INFANCY

Discovering the Real America
1980—$30,000; 1981—$35,000

Newborns require endless feeding, diaper changes, and attention to every cry, while offering the occasional smile or giggle as scant compensation. Infancy seems interminable, but no amount of coaxing, jiggling, or urging can make that infant get up and go to college. An infant has to be an infant. In the first years of a new business venture, processes that will eventually become routine must be painstakingly developed by trial and error, and progress will seem to move at a crawl.

In January, Doug Jensen and I came to a cruel realization at the same time: boot sales were seasonal, and the winter buying season lasts only a few months. In retail, buyers ordering for the next winter's sales place their orders in January and February, with an expected delivery date of around October, providing the them time to put product on the shelves before the first cold weather.

We looked at each other, and said, "We're screwed." Any thoughts of quickly selling our inventory over the summer disappeared, so we contemplated the options.

I ran the accounting for 1979. Out of the $20,000 investment from the Rhodes family, we had a loss from the advertising and overheads of $6,800; the rest of the money was tied up in inventory in my spare bedroom. Cash was our most immediate need, so we decided to try swap meets. Doug chose the Saugus swap meet in the San Fernando Valley, and I picked the Orange County swap meet near Newport Beach.

We loaded our vans on Fridays, then every Saturday and Sunday we got up around 4 am and drove to the swap meets to pull into lines of waiting vehicles. The gates opened at 8 AM, setting off the mad scramble to find a spot and set out product. On a good day—when there were only fifty cars in line—we got spots near the center of the action. A bad day had us on the perimeter with almost no foot traffic.

If the weekend was sunny and mild, we sold only one or two pairs a day. Yet when it was cold and squally, we sold ten to twenty pairs a day. I applied this lesson when doing my rounds to surf shops. I knew better than to visit retailers on hot, sunny days, when sheepskin was the last thing they wanted to see.

After we'd worked the swap meets every weekend through the end of March, Doug came to the conclusion that we had both gone into the boot business with thoughts of instant riches but, based on our first season, that obviously wasn't going to happen. He asked me if it would be okay if he pulled out of the venture. One of his swap-meet customers had offered him a good job in the film-editing business, a field that resonated with him. It was an opportunity too good to let pass. Since the hot Santa Ana winds from the desert had begun, heralding the end of winter for Southern California, we knew we'd both have to find jobs anyway, so we high-fived each other and went our separate ways—at least regarding the business.

Over the summer, the folks at *Action Sports Retailer* had decided that the fledgling industry needed a trade show, hoping to mimic the huge success of the Ski Industry Association's shows in Las Vegas. They canvassed all of their advertisers to sign up for the first show, to be held in March at the Long Beach Convention Center.

I called Country Leather and asked George to send me a few sheepskins and some Australian tourism posters to help decorate my ten-by-ten booth. On my left was a booth for Gordon and Smith, one of the biggest surfboard brands and surf accessory distributors at that time.

All of the big brands of beach culture were represented at the show, from Hang Ten, Stubbies, Body Glove, and Catchit to Gotcha, Lightning Bolt, Hobie, Vans, Ocean Pacific, Rainbow sandals, and sunglass companies like Scott, Vuarnet, and Style Eyes.

I felt almost apologetic for being in the same show as these companies that, to me, represented the pinnacle of success. I had to wear my game face to hide my embarrassment as I wheeled my boxes of sheepskin boots into an environment dominated by sun-and-sand products.

I hired a friend, Debbie—young, blond, in shape, and cute—to model the boots. For two days we stood or paced or just sat around, hoping to make big orders. It finally dawned on me that most of the buyers didn't actually place orders at the show. They came by the booths to look over the product lines to see what was new, chat with their regular sales reps, and set appointments for the reps to come to their stores and take the orders.

Since Doug had moved on, I realized I needed to acquire some kind of sales team or I'd have to do everything myself. Since it was common for sales representatives to carry more than one brand at a time, I asked the sales reps at the Gordon and Smith booth next to me if they'd like to carry a sensational new line of sheepskin boots. They laughed.

If these guys are such elite salesmen, I wondered, *why aren't they jumping at the challenge of pioneering sales of a new brand?* The question was also the answer: No successful sales group wants to take on the hard work that breaking in a new product requires.

The few orders I wrote during those two days of the show didn't make up for the cost of being there, yet I was happy I had at least exposed the

UGG brand to the retailers covering the surf market in California. Maybe when I came around on my sales circuit, someone would say, "Oh yeah. I heard of UGG somewhere."

Sales reps are the rubber on the road for any business with an extensive product line. Repping can be a fulfilling career, but it has its dangers. A rep's success is ultimately measured by the relationships each one has within their customer base. Those starting out will have a limited base of customers, so they have difficulty representing established brands that have traction in the marketplace. Because of this, they usually have to pioneer small brands and bring new products to the marketplace. Conversely, established rep groups have developed strong customer bases and shun the amount of time and work necessary to pioneer new brands.

A new rep will generally carry several brands and products serving their customer base simply to make ends meet, but eventually, as they gain traction and as the brands grow, they can reap the rewards of all the work they put in over many seasons. However, one of the seemingly unfair aspects of the business happens when they are so successful that their commissions become so large (often exceeding the pay of the CEO of the business itself). When that happens, there is a tendency for the brand owners to take over their best customers to be handled "in house" leaving the rep who did all the hard work back on the street with the smaller customers. When I left Australia to begin the UGG business, I thought salesmen were only found in used car yards. Now, however, with many miles and years of selling on the road, I have the utmost respect for this niche of businesspeople, who are at the root of most successful businesses.

But for now, how was I going to stay alive through the rest of the year?

The money I'd made from the sale of my rental house in Perth was almost gone. I called Pete in Perth to ask if he would consider selling the house we co-owned. He agreed to contact a realtor and put the house on the market.

I always carried a full run of sizes of boots in my van, so every time I went surfing in Malibu I could open the back doors and be open for business. I made a lot of friends that way and soon acquired my nickname, the UGG guy. My surfer friends raved about the boots to their friends, generating a surprising amount of word-of-mouth marketing.

As frustrating as it may be, there's no way to accelerate the period of infancy a new business must go through. Do you look at a baby in a carriage and anguish over the fact that he or she isn't yet in college?

The surest way for a tadpole to become a frog is to enjoy every day being a tadpole.

Occasionally, a product like the Pet Rock will have instant and widespread success, but these types of fad products are short-lived. In today's online market, products like phone apps and other downloadable products can become overnight successes, but most tactile products still need some time to gain leverage in the market. Sheepskin boots are, of course, a tactile product; the endurance of the UGG brand was cultivated by every person who experienced the feeling of sheepskin caressing their bare foot, and raved about them to their friends.

I know now that even if I had been able to launch a million-dollar marketing campaign that first year, the increase in sales over the slow, word-of-mouth process would have been minimal. The growth of a product's reputation and market is organic. The only way to get through the infancy of a new business is to wait it out, clean up the messes, and let it grow toward maturity.

Life at my house in Santa Monica was frugal. I often went to the local Chinese restaurant on Monday and bought two spicy dishes. One I ate there, the other I took home and split into four plastic bags. On Tuesday, I bought a week's worth of fresh vegetables for a stir-fry, and each night I heated up the fresh veggies and threw in a leftover Chinese pack, stretching one meal to cover the rest of the week. Ironically, this frugal diet kept me probably the healthiest I've ever been.

Through my roommate, I found a job with a buddy of his who had a boat-cleaning business at Marina Del Rey. Every morning we showed up at the dock, and for long, pleasant days that drifted into months, I washed, scrubbed, wiped, polished, and vacuumed the flotilla of boats resident at the marina, even scraping off the algae that built up below the waterline, a chore that was actually less unpleasant than it sounds.

Through Margot, I met a building contractor, and halfway into the summer I jumped ship from the marina and doubled my wages working as a laborer on construction sites in Bel Air. I worked on some of the most exclusive homes in one of the wealthiest suburbs of L.A.; just driving in and out of the Bel Air gate each day made me feel like a millionaire—not a bad mind-set to be able to find when your business is still in its infancy.

• • •

The second bedroom of my new apartment on Narragansett Avenue in San Diego's Ocean Beach became the UGG warehouse, with an unpainted door laid flat across two filing cabinets to serve as my desk. It was fall, and time to get back on the road selling.

By now, buyers were familiar with the UGG brand from trade shows and from the small ads I had ran. Some of them had asked me to come by their stores.

In every area where I had an appointment, I'd pull into the local gas station, find the pay phone, and check the yellow pages directory for surf, ski, and sporting goods stores to add to my list. My dread of cold calling was still very powerful, but I had learned that it was pointless walking into a store and showing boots to a store clerk. I was now much more sophisticated! I would drop a quarter into the pay phone and ask if the buyer was there. If he was, I'd get them to tell him the sales manager of UGG would be stopping by in a few minutes. This method forced me to make the visit, and the fact that I wasn't showing up unexpected made it a little easier walking into the store, humbly apologetic for wanting them to stock sheepskin boots in a surf shop.

I always felt the easiest way to deal with a distasteful chore was to put it off. However, I found that delayed tasks all ended up in my subconscious filing cabinet, and ultimately the mental pressure of undone tasks outweighed the pain of doing them in the first place. Now I periodically list all my tasks on a page and I put a date next to each item to have it completed. Just putting them in writing eases the mind and somehow they all get done.

In October, November, and December of 1980, the phone rang every day with calls from retailers reordering.

Each weekend I set up a display at the swap meet at the San Diego Sports Arena and prayed for cold, cloudy days. I was beginning to enjoy myself and found that I got a lot of customers who had heard from friends that they should try these boots. "Friends of friends" was becoming my most powerful selling tool.

By the end of January 1981, the phones fell quiet again, and fill-in orders were sporadic. I tallied up the invoices and discovered that, although sales for 1980 were almost $30,000, we had to pay $20,000 to buy the product from Country Leather, leaving a gross profit of $10,000. Since the year's expenses for advertising, trade shows, and road expenses exceeded this, we ended the year with a small loss. I hadn't paid myself a salary, and with the business winding down for the season, I began to look for work to pay my bills and my increasing credit card balance.

With a big local drug culture left over from the sixties, Ocean Beach had become a depressing place to live. Every morning when I went for a jog, I dodged beer cans and broken liquor bottles. The surfing was great, but it was even better up at Pacific Beach a few miles north. So I rented a place up there and moved the UGG warehouse into the spare bedroom.

In February, I had just enough credit left on my card to reserve space in *Action Sports Retailer*'s trade show (ASR) at Long Beach. I began preparing samples and order forms, cards, decorations, electrical cords, and what seemed a hundred other things to make the booth work. I had no idea that I would be doing this four times a year, in various locations, for the next fifteen years.

George sent new samples where the rough-stitched seams were now covered by a nylon binding that made for a very clean bond to the soles. We were occasionally getting glue on the uppers, but this was a huge breakthrough in product development, and I realized that I should have been more proactive in demanding better quality form George. From that time forward, we began a series of improvements every season to satisfy the American consumers' desire for the best.

The exhibitors and attendees at the show had doubled since the first year, and although business was slow, a steady stream of new retailers placed orders because they'd heard good reports of *sell-through*—the amount or percentage of the product sold relative to the amount available in the store—from the shops that carried UGG the previous season. My baby was beginning to crawl.

Again, I asked the sales reps from Gordon and Smith if they wanted to carry the UGG line. Again, they laughed.

In March, we made our first foray into the ski market at the Snow Show in Las Vegas, an overflow show for small companies that couldn't get into the main ski-industry event at the Hilton Convention Center. With very little traffic, the show was a disappointment. There was no interest whatsoever in our boots. Most of the people who came by told us that sheepskin wouldn't be practical in their locations because of the mud and slush and so on. Although I was tempted to tear the booth down and leave town early on the last day, the mantra I'd learned from a book called *Success Through a Positive Mental Attitude* by Napoleon Hill and W. Clement Stone kept me going: "Always be prepared to go the extra mile."

The mantra definitely paid off as, finally, one buyer ordered sixty pairs, the single largest order we'd received since launching the business.

This Snow Show was a total bust for another new vendor, a young guy with long hair who had set up his own pitiful display, which consisted of just a video machine sitting on a rented table. I became aware of him as I helped my friend Steve Foulger set up a booth to introduce Rollka grass skis to the industry. Besides big, glossy photos of grass skiers making turns on European slopes, we had a video machine showing a looping film of the Italian Olympic snow ski team running gates down a huge, green, grassy slope in Italy.

As the show got underway, we drew a good crowd with our Italian video. Every now and then, we walked past this young kid's table and lingered to watch his movie, which was of himself dragging a pointy-nosed board up a snowy hill that might have been in his backyard. At the top, he'd turn the board around, stand on it, pick up the rope to raise the nose up, and push off down the hill. Turn, turn, turn, turn . . . until he came to a stop at the bottom of the hill. And then he picked up the rope and dragged his board back to the top, over and over again.

We turned away to chuckle, so as not to humiliate him. We were the sexy grass-ski team, and here he was, trying to create a new sport that involved riding a homemade sled standing up. We slapped each other on the back and walked away, feeling sorry for this misguided kid.

His name was Jake Burton. He would go on to be one of the founders of snowboarding and head up an international corporation worth hundreds of millions of dollars. A classic example of "You can't give birth to adults."

• • •

On the freeway back to San Diego, I wondered where I was going to find work to carry me through the summer.

Updating the accounting was depressing, and collecting money from slow-paying customers was a grind. Summer was approaching, and I knew there would be no new sales until September. I called a meeting with our investor, Mack Rhodes, to discuss our situation. We agreed that we would need more capital before the next season started. I was down to eighty bucks in the business bank account.

I called Pete in Perth, who was just closing escrow on the sale of the house he and I co-owned. With my $10,000 proceeds, I had some breathing room. I meditated and wrote out my first ever positive affirmations, and eventually felt a new spiritual lightness, a sense that things were going to work out.

> *My affirmations early on were simply items on a page with a heading at the top that said "Priorities." On a daily basis, I had so many projects and details flying around in my head I was always feeling overwhelmed. Every few months I would put them in a list as projects to complete, and just this simple act of seeing them all at once on one sheet made them seem less burdensome. I would start out with the big items, such as raising money, new product ideas, trade show ideas, and then end up with personal items, such as keeping healthy and vowing to stop chewing my fingernails. I wasn't calling upon the universe to fix anything at the time, but now with my understanding of how Spirit works I have a whole new appreciation of praying to my Higher Power and the peace that comes from every meditation.*

In August of 1981, I met Matt Fisher, the brother-in-law of one of my best friends, Ross Johnston, from Australia. Matt offered me an unusual job that paid $1,500 for one month's work. His business partner was John Buser, a guy who had the ability to see value in things that nobody else wanted; he'd buy them cheap, tweak them in some way, and flip them for huge profits. This was the era when huge mainframe computers used by corporations were being replaced by the first desktop computers; the mainframes were the size of refrigerators, presenting a logistical problem for the corporate accountants who just needed to get rid of them.

What John knew (and nobody else had yet figured out) was that every connection inside that mainframe, where one wire met another or a memory chip was socketed to a motherboard, was coated in gold.

Matt and John had bought hundreds of mainframe computers cheaply and stored them in several states, where they were waiting to be dismantled. They provided me with a hammer, a screwdriver, a pair of wire snips, the rental of a huge green station wagon, $2,000 for expenses, and a plane ticket to Milwaukee—my first stop on a route that would also take me to Chicago, Indianapolis, Cincinnati, Detroit, Pittsburgh, Baltimore, and Philadelphia.

The warehouses in each city were generally in the industrial suburbs, where I arrived, tool bag in hand, to perform my routine. I cracked open the computer cases like a surgeon cracking open a ribcage, and began to strip the internal organs from each unit. As I left Milwaukee heading south to Chicago, I was struck by the difference in vegetation of the Midwest. Instead of the brown hills of a California summer, everything here was green and lush.

Until this summer job driving across the Midwest, I had thought that California was typical of America, but forever after, I understood that the heartland of America is vast and abundant with sights and experiences to treasure, and that California is, in so many ways, a different country.

My last assignment was at a moving and storage company under the Cross-Bronx Expressway in New York, operated by a ragtag bunch of Irishmen who had collected about one hundred computers. The night before my last day, Neil Brezner, one of the owners of the company, invited me to stay at his home. My heart sank as I imagined sleeping on a threadbare couch in a cramped tenement in the Bronx, drinking beers and eating pizza, but his gesture was so kind that I accepted the invitation. He wrote down the directions on a scrap of paper, which I stuffed into my pocket.

To my surprise, while following the directions the next day, I found myself outside the city, driving north along a beautiful river through pleasant countryside, wondering if I had somehow taken a wrong turn. I pulled in at a shopping center, Neil came to meet me, and I followed him a few more miles up winding roads where handsome houses peeked out from among broad old trees and elegantly landscaped gardens. Each home was a two-story redbrick structure with huge white columns framing a portico. Some houses had white stone lions at their entrances. We pulled into the driveway of the largest house, where Neil introduced me to his wife and three teenage daughters.

That evening, instead of pizza and beer, we sat down to a long table set with fine cutlery and dinnerware, and ate steaks and baked vegetables as classical music played on the stereo. I learned that the girls were enrolled in an exclusive school and Neil's wife was active in country club activities. The following morning, despite my lack of religious persuasion, I went with them to my first Catholic mass before bidding them farewell and heading for my flight home.

So ended my second immersion into American culture. In just four weeks, I had been exposed to a diverse and astonishing America that few Australian tourists ever see on their vacations.

I was blessed that I had trips like this to expand my horizons, and even more so for the many places the UGG business took me to in racking up nearly two million frequent flier miles. One of my great desires is to travel as much of the planet as possible before I die. This is such a diverse world, and only by travel can you experience how different yet alike people are. Building a business—or working for a salary—is important, but I doubt the last thing I wish before I die will be that I spent more time at work. Sure, you have to pay the bills and set something aside for the rainy days, but the secret is to find joy every day in some part of your work that energizes and inspires you, so that what you do daily is not really working.

I also vowed that I would try to never again judge people based on my preconceptions.

Back in San Diego, I was on hand to open all the boxes I had shipped and somehow, without planning to, I spent the rest of the summer working in the computer scrapyard.

• • •

The first rainstorms hit the California coast in October and November, and the phones began ringing again. Mack Rhodes and I pooled enough money to send a letter of credit to Country Leather, and thirty-seven cartons arrived a few weeks later. I made my cash on delivery (COD) stops at Mitch's Surf Shop and Jack's Surf Shop, and we were back in the cash flow again.

Originating from the Latin word *accreditivus* meaning "trust," letters of credit are used primarily in international trade for transactions from a supplier in one country and a customer in another. To induce the supplier to send product, the customer puts money into his own bank for the total price of the product he wishes to purchase, and his bank issues the letter of credit (L/C) direct to the supplier's bank. Shipping documents arrive with the product, and having been checked for compliance at customs, the documents are forwarded to the customer's bank. The customer's bank then wires the money for the shipment to the supplier's bank account, completing the transaction. Stated more simply the L/C is a bank guarantee.

The weather turned cold, and I realized that I had fallen behind in keeping track of inventory and placing orders with Country Leather. The phone orders were frenzied; I began to run out of sizes in the most popular styles. No matter how I begged George to send me emergency inventory, I got the familiar, "She'll be right, mate! We're going on vacation for six weeks, but I'll send them in February."

After the Christmas rush, I did the accounting for the year and found that, despite the bustle of activity, sales were just $35,000—only $5,000 more than the previous year.

I wondered if I should give up. I knew that one of every two people in Australia owned some sort of sheepskin footwear. What was I doing wrong here in the United States?

There's no way I'm going back to accounting, I thought. *No, I'm healthy, happy, and I have a lot of great friends. I can always find work to keep me alive and the surf is great here. Anyway, next season, UGG is going to take off!*

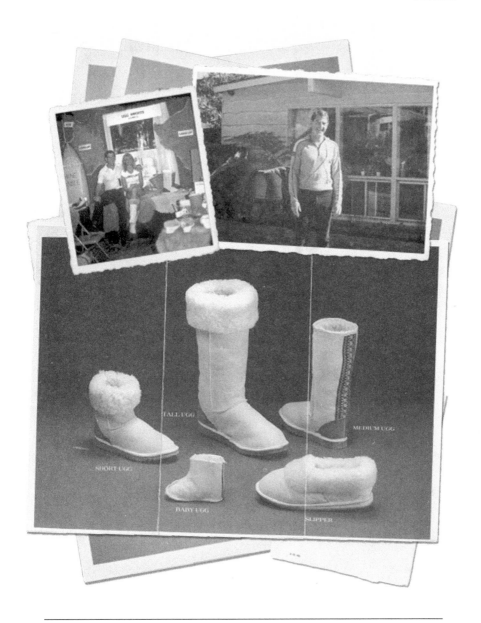

Top left: First Action Sports trade show.
Top right: Brian at third UGG "warehouse" (bedroom).
Bottom: New and improved boot samples.

CHAPTER 3

THE TODDLER YEARS

The Worst of All Business Elements
1982—$40,000; 1983—$200,000

All parents can tell hair-raising stories of their child's terrible twos, when a child's expanding reach makes us aware that dangers arise constantly—sharp objects everywhere you turn, toadstools in the lawn, the corner of a tablecloth within reach. For entrepreneurs, they can discover that despite the chaos, a new business can indeed find traction.

Nineteen eighty-two was the year I decided to give up on the UGG business.

As the 1981 winter season wound down, my lack of progress with UGG cast a shadow of doubt and uncertainty over plans that had seemed so simple a year earlier. Visions of instant riches were replaced by the dread of losing our investors' money. The $20,000 of initial capital I thought was more cash than we could ever spend had now dissipated. We'd had losses for three straight seasons.

As I didn't want to work in the computer scrapyard for another summer, I considered my options. My grass skiing buddy, Curtis McBride, was negotiating a lease of about forty hilly acres on the Gillespie Airfield property in El Cajon, and I was interested in being part of it, so I got a job as a greenskeeper at a golf course, hoping I would learn about turf management for our future slopes.

Despite having to get out of bed at 4 AM every day and be out on the course before sunrise, I loved the job and came to appreciate the thought and creativity that went into making the game a pleasant experience for the players. One of my tasks was to change the hole locations on the par-three, nine-hole course. Every morning I had to race to stay one hole ahead of a crotchety husband and wife in their eighties who teed off at dawn and cussed the ball, the sprinklers, each other, and me if I hadn't finished plugging the holes and cutting new ones. With the rest of the crew, we could install or remove a bunker, make hills from flat terrain, change the directions of the fairways, and move mature trees around. I loved working in the sun all day and knocking off in time to get home for a surf.

Over the long, hot summer of 1982, working on the golf course gave me plenty of time to consider our prospects for success, and I realized that it had most of the worst elements described in any business textbook:

- **Inventory:** In order to sell one size, we had to stock at least eight sizes of an expensive product.
- **Profit margin:** Because our product was so expensive compared with other footwear sold in surf shops, we had tremendous consumer resistance. The boots sold at retail for $80. We sold them to the stores for $40. Since our cost was $30, our gross profit was around $10, or 25 percent. I learned (many years later) that a business cannot survive long without gross profits of at least 35 to 50 percent.
- **Seasonal:** Although we made a lot of money during the three months (October through December) of the annual UGG selling season, with practically no income for the other nine months, we

couldn't afford to run an office for the entire year or hire permanent employees.

- **Receivables:** We were expected to offer thirty-day terms to vendors in the surf market and one hundred and twenty days in the ski industry. When retailers had their own cash flow problems, our invoices were the last to be paid.

As I began to sell to the bigger retail stores, I learned the term *keystone*, which is to double the wholesale price from the vendor. In our case, the boots we sold to stores for $40 were automatically keystoned to $80. The pressure was on us all the time to trim our profit margin, knowing that every extra dollar we charged would end up two dollars more at retail.

- **Cash flow:** Most of the marketing expenses occurred in the first few months of each year, including costly trade shows and acquisition of new-season samples. All the money we made during the winter was gone by March or April, leaving me to live off credit cards for six months of the year.
- **Lack of product acceptance:** Sheepskin boots were not understood in the United States. Retailers needed to actually *wear* them in their stores and then explain their merits to their customers. Sheepskins boots were just not intuitive products that jumped off the shelf.

We had a lot of inventory to move this year, and yet at ASR and the Snow Show in Vegas, even with larger booths and better decor, we got lots of lookers and few sales. Once again, I asked the guys at Gordon and Smith if they wanted to rep the UGG line. They still laughed.

Just like no amount of pushing or nudging can make a newborn infant stand up and start running, our UGG toddler was still in its crawling stage and it had to have that time. I was continuing my road trips, doing all the right shows, sales presentations, and advertising, yet nothing appeared to be happening.

Demoralized, by the end of the summer, I decided to sell off the remaining inventory stacked in my bedroom, shut down UGG, and concentrate on grass-skiing development as my full-time career.

And then, fate stepped in with two seemingly unrelated but life-changing events.

Residents of a new housing development on the boundary of the Gillespie Airfield banded together and pressured the city to reject Curtis's application to lease the hilly property for grass skiing.

At around the same time came the first stormy days of mid-September. I arrived home from the golf course damp and tired to find dozens of messages from surf shop buyers clamoring for inventory and even offering to drive to San Diego to pick up their orders! With COD invoices in hand, I began collecting cash flow for the new season. Just like that, I was out of grass skiing and back in the boot business!

Even though I knew that UGG had all of the worst elements, our regular customers had an infectious enthusiasm for our boots. I kept telling myself it was just a matter of volume. If I could build the sales enough, I would have money left over to weather the summer expenses and still be able to afford new inventory for the coming season.

George at Country Leather was now comfortable enough with my payment history to send me inventory on his own credit, so I filled-in sizes we were light on in the warehouse in anticipation of strong sales.

Why does a new entrepreneur carry on in the face of losses and not paying him/herself a salary? Let me introduce *contribution margin* accounting. If you sell your product for $30 and it cost you $20 to make, then your profit margin is $10. This $10 margin offsets expenses beyond just the cost of the product. Stated another way, if the warehouse rent is $750, then the profit from seventy-five items will pay that bill. If your advertising is $300 for the month, then the profit from thirty items will pay that bill. The same goes for car payments, gas, employee salaries, and every expense that goes into running the business.

Now, new entrepreneurs, being generally optimistic, simply think that selling more next year will solve the problem. And if the expenses didn't grow to meet the higher volume, they'd be right. Eventually they figure out how to budget and plan and one day even include their salary.

* * *

Although every store that had carried UGG product the previous year reordered, it was hard work to convince new stores to buy. I needed an incentive to get new stores to put the boots on their shelves, just to see if customers bought them.

Sales growth was also stymied by the fact that Americans believed that wearing the boots required socks and that sheepskin was delicate, hot on their feet, and useless when wet. We not only needed to get the boots displayed on store shelves, but we also needed store staff to have actual experience wearing them. I knew that if a potential customer asked the sales clerk what UGG brand boots were like and the clerk had no idea, then no sale would happen. Yet I knew people who already wore them were quick to praise them to everyone they met.

What we needed was a sheepskin-boot evangelist in every store.

I had an aha moment and I felt the goose bumps crawling up my arms. I created a program called "The Six-Pair Stocking Plan": for every store that bought six pairs, I gave a free pair to the store manager to wear in the store.

I got back on the road with new enthusiasm. I asked each store manage to try on a pair of boots without their socks. Their positive reaction was universal, and soon I was opening up new accounts on every trip.

The sporadic advertising I had been doing needed to become an organized, full-on campaign. In *Action Sports Retailer* magazine, I ran ads publicizing the Six-Pair Stocking Plan, featuring photos of several major stores' managers along with their quotes about the success of the product. For the consumers, I also ran ads in *Surfer* and *Surfing* magazines featuring a couple posed in boots on the rocks at Windansea Beach in La Jolla.

The new inventory overflowed the spare bedroom warehouse and spilled into the rest of my apartment. In October, the phone was ringing constantly. I transcribed orders into invoices, picked the sizes and styles required, boxed them for shipment, and did the paperwork for UPS until 9 or 10 at night. On cold days, I visited new customers and stores that had declined to buy on my previous visits.

By November's end I was exhausted, with the Christmas rush still to come. It was common for some stores to call every day with orders for one or two pairs, and as inefficient as this business model was, I knew that exceptional customer service would be the most important element in the success of the entire UGG venture. I could easily have insisted on large minimum orders, eliminating half my work, but I knew no retailer wanted to look at thirty or forty pairs of unsold boots at the end of each season. My goal was to leave their shelves empty in February.

Early on, I observed that retail buyers were a lot like gamblers, with only a limited amount of cash to play with. This cash is called *open-to-buy*. Each buyer bets that every item of inventory they buy will be sold by the end of the season, with the cash being added back to their open-to-buy for the next season's purchases. If the products have a good sell-through, they have the cash to buy all new styles and colors for the next season. If their bet is wrong, then they are stuck with old product and will have to discount it severely to get cash back into their stash. Knowing this, I was careful not to load them up with excess inventory and preferred to fill in from our warehouse even though it was a lot more work.

After Christmas, I did the 1982 final accounting to find that sales had increased by only $6,000 from the previous year.

I couldn't figure it out. I had quadrupled the advertising spending, driven twice as many road trips, instituted a smart incentive program, and put in at least twice as much time packing and shipping—yet sales reached only $41,000. I had enough cash coming in from the receivables and late COD collections to pay for the new season's samples from Country Leather and for entry fees for ASR and the ski show in Vegas, but I knew I'd be broke again very soon, living on credit cards come April.

Once again I wondered if I should give up on UGG. What kept me going was the single fact that had sold me on the soundness of the concept in the first place and had by now become my mantra: I was sure that one out of two people in Australia owned some sort of sheepskin footwear. What was I missing? What was the key? What was it that would mobilize the awesome spending power of Americans who lived the same lifestyle as their Aussie counterparts?

• • •

Nineteen eighty-three was the year that the UGG business finally stood up and began to walk. But first, I had to share with our investor that the previous year showed a loss of $2,500. Mack Rhodes didn't blame me, as I had feared. He knew I hadn't even been paying myself a salary and no one was in more pain about the matter than I was. He looked over the figures and agreed that we needed an infusion of capital. He just wasn't ready to open his checkbook and potentially throw good money after bad.

But it wasn't necessary, because again, once I put my intentions out into the universe, serendipity kicked in.

The following day, John Buser, the owner of the computer scrapyard, was at my apartment to go for a run with me, but we had to hang out awhile before we could leave; a girl, referred by a friend, was on her way over to buy some boots. She soon arrived, tried on a few pairs, picked out one she loved, and asked me for the price, which was $117 including tax. Without a moment's hesitation, she wrote out a check and then happily went on her way, wearing her new boots.

John looked at me quizzically, and said, "How much did that pair cost you?"

"Thirty-seven dollars," I told him.

He said nothing, but I could sense his horse-trader savvy going over the numbers and projections in his head.

Then he said, "How can I get into this business?"

After we'd gone for our run, I told him that if I was going to make UGG happen, I couldn't keep working two jobs. I needed a guarantee that I could pay for my personal living expenses through the next summer. I also explained that we needed a large reorder from the factory to fill in sizes and styles.

We soon reached a deal: John would guarantee a credit line of $100,000 at the local bank that would immediately go toward ordering a twenty-foot container of boots from Country Leather. In return, John would own 50 percent of the business, for which we'd form a new partnership as UGG Imports. Since the Rhodes family already owned half the business, their interest and mine would each be diluted to 25 percent to make room for John. Mack Rhodes understood it was the only way to keep the business going and preserve the value of his investment, so we began the paperwork.

In February 1983, I began a new phase of my life, basking in the security of an actual salary, a $600 per month draw from the new capital. I kicked the business into high gear, starting with the Action Sports Show in Long Beach in February. By now, the show had passed through its own infancy and toddler phases and was vibrantly growing. The exhibit spaces were pretty much taken, attendees were plentiful, and the entire floor was carpeted. We still had our little booth next to Gordon and Smith, and once again I asked the guys if they were ready to rep the UGG line. They didn't laugh, but still there were no takers. Interest in the boots was strong, and I didn't mind that we took only a few orders; I looked forward to the buying frenzy I knew would come at the fall show.

A week later we made our appearance at the L.A. Shoe Show, only to find that buyers for the traditional shoe-store market still had not figured out our category. We got no orders. We were met with the same type of indifference at the Snow Show in Vegas, although we did get repeat orders from the stores that had bought from us the year before.

In March, we moved the remaining inventory of boots from my bedroom to John Buser's scrapyard. I cut the word "UGG" from a cardboard banner left over from a trade show and nailed it over the front entrance of the building; we now had an official storefront.

Because retailers had stopped stocking winter items, I returned to the swap meets until the sunny days of California summer began in May, and I consistently sold seventy to a hundred pairs of boots each weekend.

Now that our baby was toddling around the marketplace, we had to dress it up appropriately. We commissioned John Hyatt, an illustrator from New York, to develop a more businesslike logo for UGG. The result was a powerful brand image that would come to dominate the fleece-lined footwear industry.

Around this time, my personal life took off in a new direction. I met a girl named Laura. My neighbor belonged to Torrey Pines Ski Club, which was renowned for throwing good parties. Laura's neighbor was also a member and invited her to a Torrey Pines dance at the Catamaran Hotel in Pacific Beach. I saw her across the dance floor and was immediately smitten. She worked as the personal assistant to one of San Diego's top architects, and I am forever grateful that she decided to date, and eventually marry, an entrepreneur with no money but great expectations.

• • •

I had been in business four seasons with Country Leather, and my heart rate always increased as I put box cutter to cardboard to open a new shipment. Since the beginning, every time I called or wrote to George Burcher about quality issues with his products, I was simply not getting through to him. The current boots were selling at retail but I knew the lack of consistency was unacceptable.

Finally, in an act of desperation, I searched through my inventory until I found a single boot that I would be proud to sell. I cut it in half with a pair of snips, from top to bottom, and on one half of the boot I wrote in large black letters: *This is the Minimum Quality for the US*. I sent it to George and kept the other half in my office for reference.

Immediately, the quality of the boots he was sending me went up. I could just hear him saying, "She'll be right, mate! If that's how you want 'em, we can do that easy!"

Up until then, we had just been selling whatever the factory sent to us, but this was a first step in what would become a very exact science of project management. Eventually we had several manufacturers that had to make identical products, so a very tight specification process was begun where the skin quality, patterns, thread, soling materials, and glues were all spelled out, even to the extent of packaging and shipping instructions have specific standards.

Project management can be broad in a big corporation, but for small businesses, the projects are more like "plan the upcoming trade-show," "create the new brochure," "streamline the warehouse," etc. The Project Management Institute is a worldwide body that provides a set of best practices for handling the various projects that make up a complete operation that can be extremely helpful for anyone who wants more details specifically on this aspect of business.

For the fall season, we ordered 2,560 pairs of boots, which was about 160 cartons that completely filled a twenty-foot ocean shipping container. With a little money left over in the bank ($100,000 less the $93,000 for the container order), I again felt we'd never need an infusion of investor money again. John, the Rhodes family, and I signed the partnership documents, and a new phase for UGG began.

I immediately felt better—happier, more excited, and more at ease. We could now plan ahead for a season, rather than making decisions on a day-to-day survival basis. With the new logo, I redesigned the marketing and sales brochures and planned for the upcoming trade shows. We planned a campaign to expand our Six-Pair Stocking Plan, and hired a professional photographer, who set up a photo shoot with more models posed on an idyllic California beach.

Luckily, the first storms started in September, and I came home from my rounds to the retailers with $12,000 in cash. By mid-October, we had shipped over $35,000 in sales—almost as much as during the whole year of 1982!

And then, in the midst of all this positive energy, came a calamity. Valerie and Trevor Smith from Coos Bay, Oregon, called me and said, "You can't use the UGG name in America. We own the registration for UGHS, and you're infringing on our trademark."

I agreed to meet them when they came down for the L.A. Shoe Show.

Valerie was a strikingly good-looking woman with dark skin and hair, and a flashing smile. She dominated the meeting.

I learned that she had moved from Australia to Oregon a few years earlier. Her son had won a basketball scholarship to a university in Oregon, and Valerie had visited him, bringing several pairs of sheepskin boots from Australia as gifts for her son's hosting family. Realizing that the boots were such a hit and, like me, realizing there were no manufacturers in the United States, she had set up a small boot-making factory in Coos Bay.

She ranted and threatened me with legal action. I listened, and we left without reaching an agreement.

Later at the Vegas Shoe Show in late September, a steady stream of buyers who visited our booth told us that a woman in another booth was promoting another sheepskin boot and told them not to buy from me, because we wouldn't be in business next year. Of course, I knew that woman was Valerie Smith.

Valerie was a serious distraction, but I had bigger fish to fry. It was October, and my road trips were overdue, the urgent voice mail messages from retailers confirming how overdue. I began to notice that when I walked into a store, I'd see my buyers' eyes light up and they would say, "Hey, it's the UGG guy!" After three years of humbly shuffling into surf shops to beg a few moments of their time, I realized these guys were becoming my friends. Despite my reluctance as I started out on my route each morning, by lunchtime I was always feeling good. By the end of the day, I was feeling great.

Once we began our print advertising campaign in *Action Sports Retailer* showcasing the surf shops that had taken advantage of our stocking plan, it became easier to convince new buyers to take a chance on the product. I continued my commitment to swap out sizes to assure they ended the season with a sold-out position, a promise I'd kept for two years. We began running our new ads in *Surfer* magazine, knowing we had to sell 150 pairs of boots to pay for each $2,000 four-color ad.

*Exceeding the customer's expectations has always been something
I've strived to do. I took great pains to manage the UGG inventory
in every store, making it easier for the owner to eliminate carry-over
of unwanted items with summer coming on. Getting a bigger order
next time around is much easier if the products sold out last season.*

Shipping was so fast and furious in October that we hired a stock clerk. I continued to go on the road, opening up new accounts every week. Since some of the bigger stores—South Coast Surf, Encinitas Surf, Gordon and Smith, Jacks, Newport Surf and Sport, E.T. Surf, Val Surf, and Portola Surf—began bringing in sizable orders in preparation for the Christmas rush, John Buser began to worry that we would run out of inventory and be unable to fulfill the orders. Against my better judgment, he convinced me to order another container of boots from Australia.

In January of 1984, the Santa Ana winds came in early from the desert, signaling the end of winter for Southern Californians. Boot sales virtually stopped dead by mid-January and never kicked back up until the next season.

Although sales for the season had topped $200,000, the container of boots from Country Leather was about to arrive, requiring all the profits we just made to take possession of it, and we still had to buy new samples for the upcoming season and attend trade shows in March. I had given in to John's optimism during the frantic October rush, when he convinced me to order the extra boots. In fact, we had done the exact opposite of what I was doing to manage inventory in all of the stores. Instead of having cash from the profitable selling season to use through the next summer, we ended up with a warehouse full of dead inventory that would not come alive until next September.

I told John we needed to increase the credit line for 1984 in order to keep the doors open, and the prospect of taking on additional debt began to make him disillusioned with the venture. Maybe UGG wasn't the double-your-money-overnight kind of play he had imagined.

Looking back, I can see how I once thought of business as a series of ups and downs. Now I don't believe in downs. Instead, I see all aspects of business development (financing, product development, staffing, new competition, etc.) as a series of plateaus; you either advance up to the next level or stand still. Disasters do not make you go backward unless you fail to overcome them or give up trying.

Another season had come and gone, and instead of giving up, I found I was more determined than ever to stick with it. The problems weren't any different; they were just bigger. But that simply stoked my entrepreneurial fire.

There are times when all entrepreneurs want to give up. From simply having a bad day to being faced with seemingly insurmountable problems, there is always the option to walk away. But it is not that easy. Creditors need to be paid. Employees have to be considered. Premises have to be vacated. But for me, the fact that I had induced investors to put up considerable amounts of money was my driving force to make things work, even if there was no salary to pay for my time.

Left: Ad for six-pair stocking plan. *Top right*: First UGG logo.
Bottom right: Mum and Dad at the first real warehouse at the scrapyard.

CHAPTER 4

CHILDHOOD

"Are the mice are running around under our feet?"
1984—Sales $500,000

The early years of school can be as much fun for parents as the child. Every proud grade, refrigerator art masterpiece, or miniature trophy seems a promise of future greatness, and the mere fact that they can tell the boys from girls gives them the illusion of maturity. That illusion will sometimes make you forget that this is still just the beginning.

Four pivotal events in the history of UGG happened in 1984, each crucial to what would define the UGG brand for many years to come.

I flew to New York for the shoe industry trade show, where once again we encountered Valerie Smith, who was again spreading bad vibes about UGG. We also discovered she had copied the styles, trim, and colors of our line. I considered changing the company name to Jackaroos (the word we Aussies use to refer to a person working as an apprentice on a sheep or cattle ranch), to put distance between us and UGHS. Maybe then she would back off.

On the plane back to San Diego, I realized that in order to remain the leader of the category, we had to be perceived as innovators. I immediately sent instructions to Country Leather to make changes to our line and bring in shades of browns and new braid colors up the back of the boots.

And so began a new UGG policy: Don't obsess over competitors. Get out in front early and then run faster!

Innovation is key to staying relevant in the marketplace, and this applies to large corporations as well as small companies like we were. In our case, the innovations were slow and methodical, but with today's electronic transfer of information, once cutting-edge technology companies can become obsolete in a year. You should continually scan the marketplace and study competitors to assess your own product's relevance and life span. This way you have the time to develop new innovations and be ready to implement new offerings to remain ahead of your competitors, instead of playing catch up.

Sitting in the new UGG office at the scrapyard, John Buser was reading the local newspaper when he spotted an ad for UGHS boots. Wow, Valerie was impinging on our home territory! We called the number and arranged to meet Stan Cobbold, who was acting as a sales rep for UGHS.

Stan's expansive, stylish office in La Jolla was impressive, his immaculate suit and tie downright intimidating to John and me in our jeans. He talked a good game with his visions for selling sheepskin boots in the United States. Originally from the north of England, Stan had emigrated to Australia. He'd sold used cars in Perth, and eventually got into real estate, buying options on housing lots and flipping them before he had to pay for them.

A student of the selling process, he'd come to the United States to develop a sales-training business, which culminated in his booking Zig Ziglar and

Norman Vincent Peale on speaking tours in Australia. Later, in San Diego, he became a resource for Australian companies trying to develop marketing strategies for the American market.

We convinced Stan to abandon Valerie and join us as a consultant, though the fact was we couldn't afford him. As we left the meeting, John and I were optimistic it would still be worth every penny of his fee just to have him in our camp rather than driving marketing for a competitor in the same market space before we had a chance to get established. He agreed to move in full-time to work out of a room at the scrapyard, on the condition we paint and carpet it first to suit his sense of style.

Stan's first proclamation: "We need some sex in the UGG image."

Pivotal Event 1: A Timely Ally

Preparing for the Vegas ski show, Stan Cobbold was convinced that our ads depicting boy- and girl-next-door types were never going to be noticed. He was certain we needed posters of beautiful girls to spice up our image. He selected Patty and Jenny to be the first UGG Girls.

The sport of aerobics had just taken off, and the era of models with tight bodies was just emerging. For the photo shoot, Stan had the girls dress in black spandex leggings and skimpy tank tops. We used a spectacular photo of Patty for our poster and we printed up a few hundred to take to the show.

We shared our booth with United Knitwear, and we became acquainted with Michael Silbert, the owner of the company. His knitted woolen sweaters seemed out-of-date compared to the latest in nylons, Lycra, and Gore-Tex fabrics, but his status as one of the founders of the Ski Industries Association gave him (and therefore us) priority booth space, right at the main entrance to the hall.

Nonetheless, as soon as I arrived at our location, my heart sank. The show organizers had changed the number of our booth at the last minute; all of the advertising we'd produced now pointed customers to the wrong aisle. Also, there was no way to use our curtain backdrop, so we made do with a poster of Patty taped to an aluminum pole and arranged our six pairs of boots on the table.

Within an hour, Valerie Smith, accompanied by a Ski Industry Association lawyer, was hovering in our booth declaring that she had a trademark for UGHS and that we had no right to be in the show. Her threats of a lawsuit against the Association if they let our products remain on display had the worried lawyer to the brink of having us escorted out.

Then Michael, our host, a soft-spoken Polish immigrant in his eighties, stepped into the conversation and, in his role as representative of the Association, took the lawyer aside. I overheard him patiently introducing himself as one of the founding members who had served on the board for many years. With masterful simplicity, he told the lawyer, "Sir, you work for me. I want this young man in my booth, so just make it happen."

I tried to thank Michael for his intervention, but he shrugged it off as yet another minor irritation. And yet, in the way he looked into my eyes at that moment, I had the feeling he recognized an entrepreneurial spirit in me that might have reminded him of his own early days in business. He also recognized the bluster of false authority when he saw it and clearly wasn't the type to be bullied.

When the show opened the next day, Patty and Jenny modeled for us in their black skin-tight workout pants and tank tops with the UGG logo screen printed on the front and back. They definitely drew a lot of eyes to our booth, but even so, interest in the boots was spotty. Once again, it was clear the industry's buyers had no direct familiarity with the properties of sheepskin. We heard the same comments over and over:

- "They're not waterproof."
- "They're too delicate for outdoors."
- "They're good-looking when they're clean, but we have mud and slush."
- "Our customers need rubber-soled boots."

Pivotal Event 2: The Skin Factor

On the third day, yet another buyer was going down an exasperating list of reasons why she couldn't possibly consider sheepskin boots for her store. Rather than nodding politely while trying to point out the facts, which I knew from experience would be useless in persuading her, I became so frustrated that I came close to grabbing her shoulders and shouting in her face. Instead, I cut her off and dared her to take off her shoes and stockings right then and try on the boots barefoot. She was reluctant and possibly embarrassed, but I was insistent.

"Oh my God!" she exclaimed as she wiggled her toes around in the fleece lining. "These are soooo comfortable! I could sell these as after-ski boots." She placed a large order.

This was a defining moment in our fledgling business, and it changed our sales pitch forever. I had been talking about comfort for three years, but had never encouraged the trade show buyers to experience the products' strongest selling point. Once we began including a try-on demonstration as part of our subsequent sales presentations, the likelihood of writing an order increased tremendously.

• • •

That night we got lucky again, purely by accident.

The ski show was a party week for all the young sales reps, and they let their hair down each night in the many discos that were beginning to define Las Vegas at the time. Patty and Jenny were right in the thick of the fun. They chose a disco that had just installed video cameras throughout the club relaying the action on the dance floors to giant overhead screens.

Patty was dressed to kill in a short skirt and tube top, while Jenny paired her own tube top with the tightest, tiniest white shorts I'd ever encountered. Even so, what made them both stand out in the crowd were their Tall white boots. The place was packed and churning to a driving disco beat. Midway through the evening, overheated and sweaty, Patty pulled off a dance move that ended with a leap into the air. Unfortunately, her tube top failed to participate in this final move and slipped down to her waist, baring her considerable assets. Before she could react, grappling for her top and covering up in embarrassment, her wardrobe malfunction was caught on video to the screaming delight of everyone in the disco. Over and over until closing, the shimmy-shimmy-jump was replayed on the overhead monitors and shouts of "UGG Girl!" rang out from the crowd.

Patty found instant fame as word of the UGG Girl's debut spread throughout the trade show for the remaining two days.

The day after the incident, it was standing room only around our six-foot exhibition space. The girls had no problem at all coaxing buyers to take off their shoes and socks. Everyone who owns a pair of sheepskin boots remembers the ecstasy of that first feel of fleece on their bare feet; our new try-on-a-pair innovation immediately converted into orders. In addition to our standard six-pair stocking plan, with its free-pair incentive for sales staff to wear the boots in their stores, we now introduced a twelve-pair stocking plan, and someone even convinced us to make up a sixty-pair plan that I thought (wrongly) would never be used. As fast as the girls could get boots on buyers' feet, Stan and I were right behind, writing orders one after the other.

The following day was just as active. Eventually, Stan and I packed up the booth, sold off the last of the posters featuring UGG Girl Patty to her many new fans, and filled his Volvo with the last of the display gear. Despite our exhaustion, Stan had the look of a happy salesman as he took the wheel for the long drive home. I rode shotgun, totaling up the orders with the late afternoon sun beating through the window. There came a memorable moment, as we wound our way westward through the rocky hills beyond the valley, when I turned to Stan and said, "Ninety-six thousand dollars."

In two days in Las Vegas, we'd written orders totaling nearly half the entire previous year's sales. The best news of all: we had cracked the ski market.

The bad news would catch up with us much later. The majority of buyers in the ski industry are women, and UGG had just established itself as a symbol of the sexual objectification of women as demeaning as the go-go boots of the 1960s. It would be years before buyers for large ski retailers such as REI and Adventure 16, as well as many specialty stores would meet with UGG representatives. Score one for UGHS—Valerie Smith quickly jumped into the gap with similar products free from sexist connotations.

Some say there is no such thing as bad publicity, and in a three-day period, thousands of ski industry people became aware of a brand that would otherwise have remained unknown. Additionally, we cracked open a market that had perceived UGG as impractical for their stores. We did hear feedback that we alienated some female buyers at the show. The Women's Liberation movement was getting more powerful, and we had to take that into consideration when looking at how to proceed after our sex-sells incident.

The modern entrepreneur has to remember that it all comes down to risk management and figuring out if a short-term publicity stunt will hurt or help the long-term recognition you are trying to build. Nowadays, there's desire for more inclusive and empowering advertising, which has spawned hashtags like #NotBuyingIt and movements founded around avoiding sexist advertising. The thing is, you can create an ad with people of all genders, races, and ages that still capitalizes on the idea that sex sells without being heavy-handed. In the end, it's all about what will work best for your product or service. The business climate that you're advertising in is one that requires some finesse, but that doesn't mean you have to ignore the siren song of "sex sells." It just means you have to do it with elegance.

Sex may sell, but sophistication will inspire brand loyalty.

• • •

With summer coming on, and knowing there was almost nothing for him to do, John and I had to reassess Stan Cobbold's position. We had little money, and Stan's check each month became burdensome. My own draw from the company still averaged about six hundred dollars each month, and Laura and I were now newlyweds. We had been living together for six months, and at the time, her income was covering most of our bills. I called Stan and asked to meet him for breakfast, dreading that I'd have to tell him we couldn't afford to pay him any longer.

Soon after we slid into a booth at Denny's and ordered the $1.99 Grand Slam special, Stan looked at me and said, "You know, Brian, I don't think there's much I can do for the company right now. I have another opportunity. Do you mind if I give you thirty days' notice?"

Despite the fact that I knew another month's salary for him was going to be hard to pull together, I was relieved when we shook hands and agreed to stay friends. Stan's boldness in injecting sexiness into the product's image had changed the course of our fledgling enterprise. I knew that hiring him had been one of the best things that we had ever made happen to UGG.

• • •

Most stores had sold out during the previous Christmas rush and were into their third and fourth reorders by the time the ASR got underway. For the first time, I wheeled the booth materials to our show space with my head held high, embodying the advice Steve from *Action Sports Retailer* had given me a few years earlier: "It is not how big you are, but how big you're perceived to be."

Once again, our double booth was next to Gordon and Smith. As we set our samples out on the table, a few of their reps drifted over, picked up the boots and began murmuring among themselves. I asked if they would like to rep the line for me. "Nah," one of them replied for the whole group. At least they weren't laughing anymore.

Our long-time customers were now confident they'd be able to sell all the boots they ordered, so instead of waiting for me to swing by on one of my road trips, they began placing orders now, in February, for delivery in September. For the first time, we wrote orders for more than five hundred pairs, covering the cost of the show. This was also the beginning of our ability to forecast sales for the following season.

• • •

Back home in San Diego, we regrouped. Our preseason orders were just over a quarter of a million dollars—nearly forty-five hundred pairs—and John and I high-fived each other. However, the reality that this would generate only around $45,000 profit—and worse, we wouldn't receive it until November—still left us with the problem of surviving the coming year.

At the Denver regional ski show, Valerie created havoc by handing out leaflets claiming we were infringing on her trademark and warning buyers not to expect orders placed with UGG to be filled because she was going to put us out of business. Later, one of our ski shop customers showed us a letter that Valerie had sent out to the entire ski show mailing list threatening legal action against those who bought from us.

At the end of April, UGHS's patent attorney sent us a letter stating that Valerie had done a deal with Shane Stedman, the owner of the Australian UGHS trademark, who was now claiming he had shipped boots with the UGHS brand to America prior to my starting business. (Under US trademark law, "first and continual use" determines ownership of a trademark.) The lawyer claimed that, three or four years previously, Shane had sent boots to Corky Carroll, the famous California surfer who was "testing the water" of importing and selling Shane's UGHS boots to his surfer buddies in California. What the lawyer didn't know was that Corky and I were longtime friends through our history of placing ads in *Surfer* magazine, where Corky was employed as the advertising sales manager. Shane's claim was unlikely to be backed up by Corky.

Nonetheless, in May I met with John Buser and the Rhodes family to discuss changing the name of our boots to Jackaroos. Regardless of the merits of Valerie Smith's case, the cost of fighting a prolonged legal battle could be ruinous. We had no cash in the bank. It was decided that it would be cheaper to change all of our marketing materials than to pay endless legal fees.

Pivotal Event 3: The Power of UGG

Through Matt Fisher from the scrap yard, I had become friends with Stan and Cathy Perry. Their son Curt was an avid surfer, and he and a few of his friends had recently talked me into sponsoring an UGG Surf Team; in return, they would help promote the boots among their friends.

Now, I called Curt and asked him how he would feel about riding for the Jackaroos' Surf Team instead.

"No way," he told me. "It would be cool to ride for UGG. But Jackaroos? That's a dumb name."

And in an instant, I realized the power the UGG brand had developed over a few short years of advertising and building awareness. I knew we couldn't just throw it away after so much hard work.

The importance of building a brand and policing it is critical. The value of a brand and its associated trademarks increases every time someone sees it and relates it back to your product or company. These are called *impressions*. I calculated that over the previous six years, with all of the advertising in magazines, banners at trade shows, hangtags on the product on retail shelves, even the logos on the heels of every pair of boots we had sold, accounted for millions of impressions of the UGG logo and the shape of the boots that it stood for. Imagine that if, instead of Nike, a college kid came up with the familiar swoosh for his skateboard business in the midseventies and then went out of business the same year. Would the swoosh mean anything? It is the billions of impressions and billions of Nike's dollars that have created the value of this iconic brand, and I would assume they spend millions of dollars in legal fees each year to protect it.

I approached a patent attorney named Carl Brown in San Diego, who coincidentally had family ties to Australia. He reinforced the idea of capitalizing on my efforts at branding and agreed to help us fight Valerie. He recommended we hold our course for the time being.

• • •

As summer rolled on, tensions began to surface between John Buser and I because of the cash flow dilemma. When I prepared a business plan to raise money from banks and venture capital firms, they all told me the same thing: "Those boots are a fad. The business will never last."

I even called a good friend, Randy, a student on the San Diego State University rugby team I had coached for several years who was now in the world of inventory financing in Chicago.

"You're crazy," he said. "Those things will never catch on!"

The lack of financing left John in a bad position. He had never wanted to be in a business with overhead; his idea of buying a container of boots and doubling his money immediately was not panning out. The cash available from his $200,000 credit line was dwindling, and we had a full warehouse with little expectation of sales until the weather turned. The only way he could recover his investment was to keep us alive until sales picked up again.

So he agreed to increase the Peninsula Bank line of credit on a month-to-month basis. In return for this, he would charge our company 4 percent per month on all money we drew against the line. Calculating that to be 48 percent per year, and we only made 25 percent gross profit, in my heart,

I knew our relationship as partners was doomed unless I could raise new money. As this solution would keep us afloat until the fall storms rolled in and sales resumed, I vowed to draw as little as possible from the expanded line of credit until then.

Then, no sooner had we inked this deal than we were served with a lawsuit from UGHS. Although a costly legal battle now looked inevitable, I was still determined to stick with the existing UGG brand.

Meanwhile, I was trying to figure out how we could get into the traditional footwear stores in the malls. I tried to get an appointment with the Nordstrom buying office, only to be told, "We don't see a big enough demand to invest in the brand."

In Chicago, I ran into rejection from every big-store buyer, until I got to the buying office for Montgomery Ward. After I'd given what I thought was my best sales presentation ever, the Ward's buyer just looked at me. There was a long awkward silence.

Finally he said, "Why are you here?"

Dumbfounded, I stammered, "To get an order for your California stores."

"Don't you get it?" he replied. "Stores like us are the elephants of the industry. We never move until there are mice running around under our feet."

I walked away without an order, but I left his office with something much more valuable. It finally dawned on me that, no matter how much I spent on advertising or how many trade shows I entered, UGG was never going to go mainstream until it was a smash hit in the specialty stores. The big chains were risk averse. They wouldn't carry an innovative product like sheepskin boots until it became risky *not* to carry it.

I'm sure all entrepreneurs who have developed a new or innovative product have encountered the same type of resistance. Even Steve Jobs failed when he tried to sell the first Apple processors to the Radio Shack guy. The key is to remember to service the mice and respect them as much as you do the elephants while waiting for the elephants to take notice. If you treat everyone like your most important client, you'll be in a position to have nothing but important ones.

This revelation suddenly took a lot of pressure off me. I had been beating myself up and feeling anxious that my baby wasn't already in college. It still had to make it through kindergarten.

• • •

Summer began, shipments trickled to a stop, and our new problem became the collection of money owed to us. We had extended credit to most of our bigger surf shop customers and the unwritten rule for the ski industry was *12–10*, meaning that no matter what month we shipped product, the payment date was December 10. Normally, we could handle some delay, but in cases where the shop wasn't doing well, we were strung out for months trying to collect. I imagine the payment process at a struggling sports shop went something like this:

"Do we need Rossignol skis next season? Yes, pay that one. Do we need Patagonia outerwear next year? Yes, pay that one. Do we need UGG next year? Not really. Let's hold off on paying that one."

During that summer, I had another revelation. I was surfing at my favorite break, Terramar in Carlsbad. The ocean surface was glassy, the waves were small and well-shaped, and I was enjoying the sun on my back when I saw one of my good customers paddling out. It was Bill, one of the owners of Hobie Oceanside, so I paddled across to say hello.

Bill and his brother had recently bought a store from my good friend, Bob Thomas, who operated out of a beach shack on the main Coast Highway. Shortly after buying the business, they tore down the shack and built one of the first mega surf shops, comprising two floors of the best brands of clothing and accessories, as well as a huge inventory of top-of-the-line surfboards. On my sales trips, I had watched the evolution of their business with some envy, wondering if I would ever be as successful as these guys.

Bill told me, "You're so lucky, Brian. I wish I were in your position."

I couldn't believe my ears. "What do you mean?" I asked him.

His next words changed the way I would think of the UGG business forever.

He said, "I can only make as much money as the people who will walk in the front door of my shop can spend. You have the whole country to sell to! UGG is going to be huge."

I had always felt pathetically small walking into retailers like Val Surf, Jack's Surf, and especially big retailers like Sports Chalet. They were selling a wide range of products, whereas I had only one product to sell. But after letting Bill's comment settle into my brain, I had a new self-image on every road trip I undertook from that moment forward. These stores were each only one point of sale, maybe a few more if they grew into a franchise. But I could sell to every outlet in the world that sold footwear!

E-commerce has created options in distribution so radical that, nowadays, even retail stores are not essential to the success of the suppliers. You can have a Ferrari built to your specs and then delivered to your home as easily as a bunch of flowers, money permitting. And in many instances, customers have no idea whether the company they are buying from is large or small, because what they judge is the website. Even companies that have wholesale distribution conduct much of their business online with both retailers and consumers, and the roles of the sales reps now is more to show and explain the products to the buyers, discuss trends, and share their feel for the marketplace.

Bill's insight was prophetic. Even the biggest surf and specialty retail chains nowadays are capped at a few million dollars of annual sales, while UGG has endured to exceed a billion dollars in revenue a year worldwide.

• • •

I used the summer of 1984 to find a solution for a problem that had been on my mind: merchandising. For a couple of seasons, every time I went to visit the UGG retailers, I would look around to see where they were displaying the boots. Invariably, they were tucked up on a shelf or way on top of a center display, lying on their sides and looking dejected—90 percent of the customers walking down the aisles still had no idea about our product.

In retail, every square foot of display space has to generate its maximum income, so all the hot-selling brands had priority. We couldn't afford to build UGG displays that took up floor space or shelf space, so I had two problems to solve:

- How can we show a casual dress image for UGG?
- How can we get good in-store visibility without impinging on existing displays?

The display specialists I consulted had no solution.

Then one day in a hardware store, I noticed some plastic chain and I got goose bumps. Back at our scrapyard headquarters, I constructed a display out of a two-foot-square sheet of plywood with our posters glued on each side. Our boots hung below on two lengths of chain and another strand of chain went up to the ceiling.

One of the posters was a beach shot with guys pulling on UGG brand boots after a surf. The other featured a couple, the guy in jeans and the woman in a skirt.

The retailers were stoked. Our displays took up no floor space at all, since they hung from the ceiling. At last, customers could see what cool people looked like wearing sheepskin boots!

• • •

As the summer dragged to a close, cash flow was again a big problem—and the cause of strained relations between John Buser and me. His vision of doubling his money on a container of boots had evaporated because of my insistence on using the profits to invest in growth for the next season. The cost of trade shows, travel, and accommodations, as well as buying new samples each February, was sucking up our cash. By August, it was all gone and we were dipping into the bank credit line and my personal credit cards to stay alive.

Pivotal Event 4: From the Mouths of Babes

One afternoon, I visited Rob Ard, the owner of South Coast Surf Shop in Ocean Beach. We decided to have a beer in his shop after closing, and in this relaxed setting I began explaining my frustration that the boots weren't catching on as I had expected, despite the expensive ads I'd been running in *Surfer* and other magazines.

Rob turned in his chair and yelled to a group of grommets (young surfers) in the back of his shop. "Hey, you guys! Come here! What do you guys think of UGG?"

"Those ads are so fake," one of them replied without hesitation. "The models in their ads are so unreal. They don't even surf, I bet."

Those words hit me like a brick, and instantly I knew they were right.

This was a pivotal moment in my understanding of marketing and advertising. I had been showing images that totally missed my intended audience. The essence of good marketing through advertising is to transport the reader into the scene, to make him or her want to belong in the picture. The more emotional the desire, the more powerful the ad, and the more disposed the viewer is to buy.

Rob and I continued drinking beers at a local pub, and by the end of the evening, we'd come up with a plan of action. The next day, I called the ad rep for *Surfing Magazine*, Pete "PT" Townend.

A legend in California, a former World Surfing Champion from Australia, PT was part of the very successful "Bronzed Aussies" advertising campaign. Although short in stature, he was (and still is) a giant in the local surfing community. At the time, he was the coach of the National Scholastic Surfing Association team. I'm still awed by the size of the waves he and his buddy Ian Cairns rode in El Salvador as stunt doubles for the movie *Big Wednesday*.

Automobile ad agencies are some of the best at advertising in a way that makes the viewer immediately want to place themselves in the ad. Luxury cars slide by, seemingly without a driver, inviting you to get behind the wheel. Or, if there is a driver in the ad, you can bet it is someone you want to get into the car and be with. Keeping your audience in mind is paramount when marketing. It sounds so simple, but the fact is, it's not always easy to remember—and to think from—your demographic's point of view. If you aren't getting results from your targeted audience, find out why by asking them directly or creating formal focus groups to appraise your ads.

"PT," I said, "we need to find some pro surfers we can sponsor to build some credibility for the UGG image. Do you know of any young pros who won't cost much to support and would like to be part of the UGG team?"

He arranged for me to meet Mike Parsons and Ted Robinson, amateur team members who were considering turning pro. They agreed to come on board for a small amount of cash and as many boots as they could wear.

Instead of posing them in a make-believe scene staged by a professional photographer, I decided to tag along with them on their way to recognizable surf spots, like Black's Beach and Trestles, shooting photos from a distance with my telephoto lens.

We also used a photo I took where Mike and a model were talking casually with each other. It was grainy and technically crude, but because they did not know they were being photographed, I captured them in a very natural way that surfer girls, a segment of the market we were trying to grow, would relate to.

I delivered the artwork to the magazines, then waited for the first storm to hit the California coast to kick off boot deliveries.

•   •   •

In September 1984, I reconciled the line of credit: $97 left from $200,000. But the weather was changing, orders were going out, and the phones were ringing. It wouldn't be long before the cash came in.

The next three months were a blur. The new advertising campaign was an instant success. The mountain of boots we'd been staring at all summer began flying out the door, and I scrambled to reorder from Country Leather. Each week we broke open cartons that had just arrived from Australia and shipped away their contents within days.

And then soon, it was trade show season again. We had booths in Long Beach, Anaheim, Chicago, and New Jersey. At the Action Sports Show in Atlantic City, we had a visitor to the booth who became crucial to saving the future of UGG. He was Nick Hock, owner and publisher of *Ski Business* magazine. An elderly man with a pronounced limp from an old ski injury, he spoke with a heavy Austrian accent. Nick told me he had been watching our progress with interest since our entry into the Snow Show and Ski Show markets. He introduced me to his friend, Paul Bussmann, who ran a ski-market sales group with about twelve rep groups.

In December, Paul and his wife, Maria, came to San Diego to meet John Buser and me, and we signed his group to carry the UGG line to the ski market across the country.

Sales for the rest of the season were brisk, and the reorders were great. Every time we got a fill-in order to replenish a customer's shelves, I did a mental dance, knowing one more person had bought a pair of boots, which meant that one of that person's friends would soon buy a pair too.

When I tallied up the sales for the 1984 season, we had surpassed the half-million-dollar threshold—almost ten thousand pairs!—and UGG was well positioned for a prosperous 1985 season.

I really felt that the hardest part of growing the business was now behind us. UGG had become cool. It was the breakthrough I had been working toward for six long years, and now that I knew the customers identification within the ad was such a critical element to our image, it would be much easier for me to duplicate this theme into different markets. Here we come!

Top left: Ads that blew surf market open, featuring Mike Parsons (on left) surfing Trestles at San Onofre State Beach, California. *Top right*: Parsons ad. Middle left: First poster. *Middle right*: Parsons and surfer girl ad. Bottom left: Attempts to transition the UGG image. *Bottom right*: Ad in mail-order catalog.

CHAPTER 5

ELEMENTARY SCHOOL

"Boots! We can't find UGG boots anywhere!"
1985—Sales $650,000

The long stretch of the elementary school years can give parents a badly needed sense of assurance that growth has settled into a routine and that maybe they're not incompetent after all. There's still the unblemished idealism of childhood, when a child is enchanted by fairy tales one moment yet mastering set theory and French the next. But every day brings new crises and expenses for parents, and every month is a struggle to make ends meet.

Nineteen eighty-five was the best of years and the worst of years. Neither John Buser nor I could have predicted how powerful Paul Bussmann's influence would be in charting the company's direction. Paul was a small, polite man with a habit of nodding his head to positively reinforce whatever point he was making in his thick Austrian accent.

Around 1952, in his early twenties, Paul and a friend traveled from Switzerland to New York. With no contacts of any kind and armed with only a natural salesman's personality, in a bar at the Manhattan Swiss Club's get together, Paul met the distributor for Henke, manufacturers of the first buckle-up ski boots. Starting in Henke's shipping department, he began making sales trips into New England and was soon given his own territory of the eleven western states. Setting out from Denver in his pink and white Ford Crown Victoria, twice a year he traveled a circuit of 9,000 miles, becoming a familiar face at ski shops from Aspen to Mammoth.

Soon Paul, and the other weary traveling sales reps of the ski industry decided the ski shops should come to them! They rented rooms in New York, Chicago, and L.A. Within a few years, the originators of these early ad hoc conventions formed what would become the Ski Industries Association, eventually hosting the largest trade show and convention for their industry, held annually in Las Vegas.

Paul's experience in ski-market sales and his reputation as one of the veterans of the founding of the association made him a formidable presence in the industry by the time he started his own sales group. We signed on with Paul's firm and his sales team hit the road outfitted with our product kits, price lists, and stocking-plan campaigns.

Having established the UGG image in the West Coast surf market, we decided our focus in the skiing market should be California snow skiers; it was logical to assume action-sport devotees who went to the state's beaches with their surfboards in summer were many of the same people who skied its nearby mountains in winter. Ironically, all it would take would be to convince them that the fleece-lined boots they'd come to love at the beach were just as practical in a snowy environment. Rather than staging a series of boring photo shoots featuring ski bunnies like every other ski apparel manufacturer, we decided to have some fun and crafted a crossover theme for our ads, blending surf and snow. We brought a photo crew to Snow Summit ski resort at Big Bear to shoot our pro surfers, Mike and Ted, along with Patty in a ski outfit, and a new model dressed in a flimsy cocktail waitress outfit, carrying a tray with tall drinks decked out with celery sticks and umbrellas for the boys. The theme of the shoot was "the tropics," and it was hilarious—a logic-defying juxtaposition of beach chairs under a palm tree with skiers and snowboarders. Mike and Ted were dressed only in board shorts, giving the appearance of having kicked back after a day on the waves. In the six-degree temperature, every few minutes Mike and Ted would throw off their coats, jump onto the beach chairs, and pose with the girls while the photographer clicked as many shots as he could before they succumbed to frostbite.

There is a nuance to ad impressions. It can be a boring impression that is hardly noticed and quickly forgotten, or it can be a memorable impression that not only stops you in and makes you take notice, but also one you will remember. Of all the ads we did, this is the one people tell me they remember best.

Seeing the developed film a few days later, we knew we had great shots of the ludicrous setting, the UGG logo, and boots artfully arranged in the snow. We ran full-page ads in *Ski* and *Ski Business* magazines and made a huge blow-up of the best shot for use at the Ski Show in Las Vegas.

When the Santa Ana winds of January turned Californian minds from thoughts of winter to summer, we settled into the routine of collecting money owed to us and working the trade show circuit. Many of the regular customers now prebooked their inventory for autumn, and we were even beginning to capture orders from the East Coast buyers, despite their continuing skepticism about the suitability of sheepskin footwear for their mud-and-slush environments.

The Ski Show in Vegas took UGG to a new level when Paul procured for us a booth on the main concourse of the Convention Center. Just being front-and-center gave us legitimacy. Once again, it wasn't how big we were that mattered; it was how big we were perceived to be. The most common question we got at the booth was, "Did you bring the girls?"

We had decided not to, since we wanted to court those buyers who rejected us last year, but on the first day of the show, we were approached by Misty Sprinkle, a former Miss Hawaiian Tropic, who was the coach of that sunscreen product manufacturer's cheerleading team. Misty wanted to know if, perchance, we had enough spare samples to outfit her six models with those tall, sexy white boots she'd heard so much about. Since she asked so nicely in her Southern Georgia accent, with a flutter of eyelashes, how could we say no? By default we still got great exposure, but it didn't look like we orchestrated it.

•   •   •

After news reached the southern hemisphere that UGG was selling well in the United States, a steady stream of Australians scrambled to get samples from Aussie sheepskin-product manufacturers to cash in on the excitement. We now discovered how many of them had bought booth space at the show. They had all sorts of trademark-infringing names for their boots—such as Jimbo's UGG boots and Down Under UGG boots. When I approached each vendor and advised him that I owned the US trademark for UGG, the replies were exasperatingly predictable: "She'll be right, mate! America is a huge country! There's room for all of us!"

For one or two seasons, I felt seriously threatened by these opportunists, until I realized that none of them showed up for a second trade show. Obviously, they had no idea what it took to set up a base of operations in America, let alone finance the cost of inventory or cope with the endless headaches of handling returns and reorders. I saw no tracks of their boots in any of my markets.

There was, however, one notable exception. On the second day of the Ski Show, Doug Price, the owner of Canterbury Sheepskins from Christchurch, New Zealand, approached me. He was showing his boots at the show for the second time, and I realized he was not one of the "room for us all" men. Dark, good-looking, well-dressed, and articulate, Doug made the immediate impression that he was a sophisticated international businessman. His company's core products comprised the finest jackets, coats, vests, and other outerwear made from top-quality sheepskin, and he had a long track record of successfully selling all over the world. What pleased me most, however, was that he was the only potential competitor so far who recognized that sheepskin boots would never succeed in the United States without an efficient local distribution operation and a brand image powerful enough to sustain a long-term business venture.

Rather than bragging he was going to drive UGG into the dust, Doug Price surprised me by offering to become our supplier. And after a few meals and a good many beers, we eventually agreed it would be all right if he cobbled up some samples and sent them to us for review. Even so, listening to Doug's ideas, I was acutely aware of my relationship with George Burcher at Country Leather as our main supplier, so Doug agreed to keep the discussion on a strictly noncommittal basis.

• • •

After the Ski Show, John Buser, and I met to discuss the future of the company. After accounting for the whole year's expenses for 1984, we showed another loss, this time climbing to $78,000, plus $36,000 interest accrued on John's guaranteed line of credit. His dream of doubling his money on containers of boots was now dead as a doornail, and I knew his main thought was how he could get his money out.

Our inventory was low, trade show costs and advertising had drained our cash, and we had just outfitted twelve new reps with samples of every new product in the line, items that would have to be deleted from sellable inventory. Despite all the enthusiastic vibes at the trade shows, the orders that poured in, and the increasingly positive reports from our customers, the account books told a different story—with no cash reserves and no cash flow, UGG simply wasn't going to survive.

Everyone reacts to the universe around them from their own unique position at its center.

We are all looking out for ourselves first. From my center of the universe spinning chaotically around me, I was at last succeeding at firmly establishing and growing a sustainable business. From John's point of view, he was watching a slow-motion train wreck, which made him intensely eager to cash out while he could still recoup something of his investment. He was adamant that he would absolutely not provide additional financial backing to buy more boots. He was interested only in liquidating our current inventory.

Our partnership was over, leaving me to find some way for UGG to survive without John's support. As I left the office, my head was swimming with doubt and fear. We had just come off a runaway Christmas sales season, and the prebookings from all the trade shows were our best ever. Why didn't John see the same potential I did? Why wasn't he willing to support us? Was he thinking of shutting down the business? Was he trying to force me and the Rhodes family out, so he could reap the rewards all by himself? Our shipping clerk told me he had overheard John having phone conversations with Valerie Smith. My confusion was beginning to run to paranoia, marking the beginning of six months of fitful sleep and debilitating neck tension. I felt as though my whole universe was under attack.

In the meantime, we continued business as usual under a façade of calm and confidence. I tried to draw the absolute minimum on the company's credit line to see us through a long, lean summer. Laura was still working and paying most of the household bills, and I again began to paper over our deficit at home with credit-card charges.

The office was busier than ever. We were training new sales reps, keeping the running tally of orders, taking calls from creditors, and talking them into deferring those never-ending payments. I finally saw the necessity of writing a business plan. We needed to have a plan to show potential investors, as I saw this as our only hope of recapitalizing the company.

On Sundays, I listened to *A Prairie Home Companion* on PBS while I did the accounting, figuring out who owed us what and how much we owed everyone else. I looked forward to Sunday lunchtimes with my ledgers spread around me while Garrison Keillor's soothing voice took me on an imaginary radio tour of the American Midwest I had grown to love during my summer dismantling mainframes. Somehow, Keillor's colorful stories managed to put life in a proper perspective.

Apart from those few comforting hours, I was constantly beset by a sense of dread that came over me every weekday morning as I opened my eyes, and haunted me every night in restless sleep. How were we going to get boots made in Australia unless I could raise money based on a persuasive business plan I wasn't sure I could write? Every night in the dark, my mind played an endless loop of minutely detailed, step-by-step scenarios: locking the offices and handing over the keys, calling customers to give them the sad news we were out of business.

During this summer of 1985, I acquired one of the most valuable tools of my life, a practice that I continue to this day. I subscribed to a monthly booklet of business wisdom called Bits and Pieces. *One of the stories recounted the experiences of Thomas Edison's wife, who described how her husband went to bed every night with a pad and pen next to his pillow. Every time he had a thought, he wrote it down in the dark, so he could then put it out of his mind.*

I tried this, with astonishing results. As soon as I wrote a horrifying fear or a potential brilliant solution down on my pad, it was flushed from my mind and I was able to relax. Despite often being unable to decipher my scrawl the next morning, I began to sleep restfully, awaking to realize the scenarios that were so dreadful in my fitful half-sleep seemed inconsequential in the light of day.

• • •

Orders were coming in from the reps at an alarming rate. Big 5 Sporting Goods had just signed on for fifteen hundred pairs. I was sending orders to George at Country Leather for deliveries beginning in September, yet I had no idea how we were going to pay for them when they arrived. John refused to budge on his position and was openly encouraging me to find new investors.

In June, with my completed business plan in hand, I presented the virtues of our product and the forecasted profits to the manager of the Peninsula Bank. He said no, as did half-dozen other banks. My wealthy friends said no. Friends of friends said no.

"You're crazy; those things are a fad" was the common refrain.

When I approached Stan Foster, owner of the Hang Ten brand, he told me he was making five million dollars a year from simply licensing the Hang Ten name, and he urged me to do the same. But I couldn't see how that would apply in our current situation: What value was there to the brand name of a failing operation?

Scouring my brain for potential investors, I even sent the plan to my cousin Dick Smith in Australia.

I first visited Dick in Sydney when he was twelve (I was ten) and he had his own neighborhood business repairing radios. When he was seventeen, he stayed at our holiday house on the coast at Moruya Heads, south of Sydney. He owned a green Morris Minor with a twenty-foot whip antenna bolted to the rear bumper. He and his friend, who had a similar setup, would talk on the CB radio with each other. (Citizens Band radios were illegal to the public at the time, licensed only to truckers and taxis and the like.)

In his early twenties, Dick opened the doors to Dick Smith Electronics. Installing car radios and later importing and selling CB radios, he built a national chain of consumer electronics retail stores across Australia and eventually sold them to the Woolworth organization for a reported twenty million dollars.

Dick was a great promoter with a magic touch for getting into the spotlight. Before dawn on April 1, he called the radio stations in Sydney and announced he had towed an iceberg from the South Pole and was about to enter Sydney Harbor. He invited the public to sample iceberg-pure drinking water, and later he'd chop the iceberg into what he brazenly called "Dickcicles." Within an hour, thousands of spectators crowded the entrance to the harbor to gawk at a ship towing what appeared to be a mountain of ice. It turned out Dick had built scaffolding on a barge and covered it with white plastic, an elaborate April Fool's joke.

In another bizarre promotion, he advertised that he was taking reservations for a flight to the South Pole — but only passengers with the name Smith were eligible to board. The pilots and crew were all named Smith, the flight would leave Kingford-Smith airport, and even all the food and drink was to have Smith associations. He filled two commercial airliners that flew around the South Pole without landing, and all the Smiths enjoyed a non-stop party.

Dick is now renowned as Australia's version of Richard Branson, an adventurer as well as an entrepreneur. He was the first person to fly a helicopter around the world, became chairman of the board of Australia's Federal Aviation Authority, and started *Australian Geographic Magazine*, among many other achievements.

Regretting that I'd not stayed in touch with Dick, I called him and asked if he would be interested in backing my venture. A week later, after reviewing the business plan I sent him, he chose not to invest, but he did offer his advice. "If it hasn't worked in the first six months," he told me, "it's never going to work. So just drop it."

My business plan documents in those early stages were eighty pages of product photos, forecasts, staffing plans, market potentials, staffing ramp-ups, recent successes, and every other piece of blue-sky belief that would entice investors to get on the bus. What I did not realize then was that investors are primarily interested in one thing: how can I get *off* the bus, with my capital intact and a good profit?

Business plans are invaluable inside the company, so that management and staff are all in alignment with the goals to become successful, but investors only want to see three or four pages of the highlights of how much money is being requested, what the company's advantage is in the overall market, and when and how they can exit.

Of all fears, the fear of the unknown is the most debilitating. The mental pressure from not knowing if the business could survive, added to the pressure of how to make ends meet at home, became so unbearable that I had to find some release in physical activity. I developed a routine of hard physical workouts to keep some balance in my life. Every afternoon for months, I got on my bike in Pacific Beach (elevation 22 feet) and rode north to the base of Mount Soledad in La Jolla. Then, without stopping, I pumped to the top (elevation 822 feet) and arrived physically exhausted but much clearer mentally. At the peak, as I looked out over the Pacific Ocean and prayed, a peace would settle over me. Then I turned the bike downhill and coasted back home.

The studies that have been done on exercise being good for your brain function and mood are myriad, so I'm not going to bore you with them here, but I will say that exercise is something that I encourage everyone to do—for your mental health if for no other reason. In a workout, you work all of your fear and tension out as well, and you're left with a clearer head and focus.

We hadn't told George at Country Leather about our cash-flow problems. We kept sending him production orders based on our forecasts of the styles and sizes we needed. Eventually, he had six thousand pairs of boots on hand and was bugging me to send him a letter of credit assuring payment as soon as we took possession at the dock, because he had been borrowing from his bank to buy skins and pay his employees. His bank was threatening to cut off his credit line unless we could provide a guarantee of payment.

Then came the night I hit rock bottom. As I arrived home, my exhaustion was complete and a black cloud of emptiness hovered over me. I felt isolated and alone, with no business mentors to turn to. I was on the verge of tears as I explained to Laura that I saw no hope for the future of UGG. Eventually, we turned on the TV; she was on the couch, and I was lying on the floor to relieve my back and neck pain that had become chronic by now. After the show finished and we turned off the TV, I rolled over onto all fours and began crawling to the bedroom. Normally a quiet person, Laura suddenly boomed at me, "Don't you dare crawl to the bedroom! You get up now and walk like a man!"

That's all it took. Something inside me clicked, and I felt the urge of my spirit telling me that there was more to life than business. Relief washed over me as I pulled myself upright and stood and walked to the bedroom with my head high.

That night was my turning point. I slept like a baby.

The next morning, I called Paul Bussmann and told him, "Paul, I hate to break this to you, but we're not going to be able to ship any of the boots your sales team have written orders for. In fact, we're probably going to have to shut down the business."

After a long silence, he said, "Don't do that just yet. Let me make some calls."

The next day, he told me that an associate of his, Neil Fearing, might be interested in buying the business. I told John Buser this news, and he said he would be willing to sell off our existing inventory, cut his losses, and let me pursue the UGG business without him.

Then I violated the first rule of negotiation: When you have a good deal, *shut your mouth*!

I started telling him how pleased I was with his decision and stupidly began describing all my nefarious scenarios of how I was going to keep UGG alive despite him if he didn't cooperate. I watched his face harden and I became aware of a weird look in his eyes.

When John came into the office the next morning, it was war! Looking at me with cold eyes, he informed me that he had reconsidered his offer. Now, not only did he want to be cashed out of the inventory immediately, he also wanted back interest and a significant royalty from the ongoing sales.

Often, our greatest fears are those which never come true. Had I shut my mouth and not reeled off my imagined fears, they would have gone away, but the very act of giving voice to them made them materialize. I had no option now except to hope that the new investor would go along with John's terms.

The following day, Neil Fearing arrived. A diminutive figure with a receding hairline, slightly squinted eyes, and a weak handshake, Neil did not make the best first impression, but he had a warm and friendly smile. After surveying our inventory—his first glimpse of UGG brand sheepskin boots—and discussing our costs and selling prices, he made a snap decision. He made it clear he had no interest in funding the existing company, but he would be interested in starting a new company called UGG America, buying the inventory and moving the operation to his own warehouse in Anaheim. He agreed to pay cash for the existing assets and an additional royalty of 7 percent of future sales for five years.

I learned that Neil had previously bought and sold various closeouts of ski boots and other ski equipment, and he was now operating as a distributor and sales outlet for Yamaha off-road motorcycles. His plan was to bring in a friend from Denver, Joe Makalusky, to handle the accounting and administration, and to hire Paul Bussmann to handle the ski-market sales. He then made me an offer to come aboard in a position parallel to Paul's as head of sales for the surf market.

When I tried to get him to sweeten his offer by pointing out that the UGG trademark was a valuable asset for which he should pay a premium, Neil went straight to the weakness I had long ago spotted.

"You're crazy. The trademark is of no value if the company goes broke," he told me. "My money is the only thing of value on the table."

It was clear Neil wanted nothing to do with UGG Imports, and if the entity disappeared into the mists of business history, that was a matter of indifference to him. For me, however, the survival of the UGG brand was paramount, even if it meant the sputtering out of my entrepreneurial dream to be president of a great company one day.

In order to repay John's investment, I signed a letter of intent to buy his 50 percent interest in UGG Imports using the proceeds from UGG America's purchase to pay down his debt, and agreeing to pass through future royalties until his full debt was relieved. This left the Rhodeses and I with 50 percent each of the original UGG Imports, and hopefully we would share the royalties after John had been paid off.

A letter of intent is a written agreement that spells out all of the terms of a prospective arrangement. Since it is "an agreement to agree," it is not legally binding, but it becomes the document given to the lawyers to turn into a properly binding contract. It can be done on a napkin or be quite complex, but it is the mechanism to move to the next stage in negotiations pending the final agreement.

Since Neil, Paul, and Joe needed my cooperation to teach them the day-to-day workings of the business, they offered to include me as a 25 percent owner of UGG America Inc., in addition to making me the sales rep for the California surf and *Action Sports* market. However, there was a caveat that I would not take possession of my shares until UGG Imports finalized the trademark lawsuit with Valerie Smith.

The UGG brand stayed alive, and UGG America Inc., was off to the races.

I helped Neil load the truck with all of the boots the new entity had acquired, and headed off to Anaheim to help him organize his warehouse.

We were at last able to send off a letter of credit to George, who was waiting with the orders ready for shipment. Most of what he was sending us was packed into a sea container, but we had him airfreight a few thousand pairs to us to meet our overdue deliveries. Leaving Neil to handle the customs brokers and take delivery of the new shipments, I set out on the road to sell, sell, sell.

I felt reborn! Good fortune had brought three new partners into the business, and I knew this was our final configuration—we would never need more investors to make UGG the hugely profitable success it was aching to become. The future would reveal how naïve this "knowing" was.

A few years ago, I read Richard Branson's *Losing My Virginity*. What I took away from the book was that the *one* thing that never changed, from his early days of selling newspapers on the streets of London to owning and operating Virgin Airlines, was that he never really had the luxury of not having to raise capital. In the times of building UGG, I felt like a loser for always needing more capital, but now I know that if your business is growing at more than 20 percent each year, it is virtually impossible to finance that growth with retained profits from within the business.

The first stop on my sales route, the surf shop closest to the new Anaheim warehouse, was Huntington Surf and Sport. The moment I walked in the door, the manager greeted me with, "Hi, Brian. I heard you sold your business."

"Um . . . What?"

"Yeah," he said. "I just called in to check on our order, and they said you don't own the business anymore."

"What?!"

I gave the shop's owner a hurried explanation and then rushed out the door to call Neil.

I ever so calmly said, "What the *#&!!%$@!! are you telling people? I'm still the owner of this business! You and Paul are my new investors."

From the center of his universe, Neil, legitimately calmly, replied, "No, you're not. You're not an owner until you resolve the UGHS lawsuit."

"Neil, you're crazy," I told him. "I'm out here meeting with actual customers. One of our main assets is the goodwill I've personally developed with these people—and you're back there in your office, throwing it all away by telling these people I'm not involved anymore!"

My marketing professor at UCLA once told us that if you have just bought a good business, you never *put out a sign that says "under new management." When you do, you run the risk that all of your loyal customers might begin to doubt whether all the good service they are accustomed to will still be there.*

I spent a horrible day going from one store to the next, repeatedly hearing that I was no longer an owner—it seemed like the unspoken part of this was "You're just a traveling-salesman hireling now." Dejected, I dragged myself home and immediately pulled out the legal agreement to study the exact wording.

Neil was right. Technically, I didn't actually get my stock until the suit with UGHS was history. In fact, I had not brought in three new partners. I wasn't even an owner!

When I later read Robert Ringer's book Winning Through Intimidation, *I realized the mistake I had made. He says reality isn't the way you wish things to be, nor the way they* appear *to be, but the way they* actually *are. Sometimes, no matter how much we want to believe otherwise, we have to listen to the outside factors that remind of us of the unfortunate reality we are living.*

For the next week, I retreated from life, losing myself in meditation and reading philosophical and religious books, hunting for some insight that would make sense of the recent turn of events. Had I lost the business? Was my ego too closely tied to my passion to promote UGG? How was I going to survive financially? What other job could I get?

Laura and I talked over the various options. The most appealing was to put the sheepskin boot business in the past and move on. My fondest hope was to be the president of a huge corporation one day. That now looked doubtful, but I was determined to start looking for the opportunity ahead.

Within a few days, Paul Bussmann convinced Neil that it was counter-productive to mention I had sold the business.

Meanwhile, the supply issue was a disaster. George Burcher had his factory filled to the brim with finished product, but he wouldn't ship until he had more letters of credit in place. Neil hadn't finalized the incorporation documents for UGG America, Inc., and was unwilling to put more funding in place until then. I got calls from a panicked George—his bank was cutting him off and he couldn't pay his workers. Our customers in the surf market were so frantic to get boots that they were showing up at the warehouse in Anaheim, picking through our odd sizes so they could put something on their shelves.

George issued an ultimatum. "That's it! I'm shutting down the factory! No more boots until I get money!"

Luckily, the flood of customers coming to the warehouse every day finally opened Neil's eyes to the fact that we were losing a small fortune in sales, and he worked out a deal with Paul Bussmann and Joe Makalusky, and sent off wire transfers to Country Leather. Airfreight shipments began to arrive, and I spent a week in Anaheim working until midnight every night to pick orders from inventory for shipping.

In November, I did my rounds of the surf shops from south of San Diego to the Central Coast, as part of my continuing service to manage their inventory by swapping out slow-moving sizes for more popular ones. Everywhere, sell-through was good. It was also great to walk into shops that didn't carry our boots to be told that customers had been asking for UGG. Many of these shops wanted to write orders, but I was so worried that our late shipments wouldn't even satisfy our existing customers that I just told them, "Come see us at the trade show in February."

This trip convinced me that further on-the-road direct sales visits were unnecessary that season. I went back to the warehouse and spent my days helping Neil do the shipping and organizing the incoming inventory, attaching UGG hangtags on boots, filling outgoing boxes, and even doing rush deliveries myself.

I noticed Neil's attitude toward me was changing. At first, he had seemed to tolerate me as part of the baggage that came along with the acquisition of an existing business, and he had little time to listen to my suggestions. Gradually, he was becoming more impressed with the efficient systems I had put in place and with my customers-first commitment. As the weeks went by, he gave me more freedom to help out where I saw a need, and I started to feel more comfortable with my role.

Around that time, I received my first commission check, which was more than $5,000—more money than I had ever seen from the business, and I was just a sales rep! Within a couple months, I found myself opening commission checks for more than $10,000, and I began to wonder whether my huge disappointment in discovering that I had recently lost the business was in fact becoming a great blessing. I paid off all my credit cards, and Laura and I enjoyed the luxury of a household budget surplus for the first time since we married.

• • •

By late December of that year, kids were telling their moms, "Everyone at school"—in other words, the cool kids—"has UGG boots. I want a pair for Christmas." It was pretty clear that our surf advertising campaign featuring Mike Parsons and Ted Robinson was an absolute success.

Unaware that sheepskin boots were primarily a surf-shop item, moms were walking into the malls asking at Nordstrom, Kinney's, Foot Locker, Thom McAn, and even Montgomery Ward, "Do you have those UGG brand boots?"

During the Christmas buying season, every local TV news broadcast assigns roving reporters to cruise the malls, poke their microphones under people's chins, and ask what is hot for Christmas that year.

In 1985, the response was, "UGG! We can't find UGG boots anywhere."

At year's end, Neil ran a report and found that sales had totaled $650,000—more than twelve thousand pairs. I'm certain we could have sold another five thousand if we'd had the stock.

I was beginning to learn there was a lot more than sales that goes into making a successful business. Having the capital or profit cash flow to pay for inventory was just as critical. Like any machine, all of the elements have to be in tune for maximum performance.

Crossover surf/ski ad with Ted Robinson (left) and Mike Parsons (right).

CHAPTER 6

PRETEENS

"How many stores should we sell to?"
1986—Sales $1.4 million

The youth who has been a big fish in a small pond begins to look around and see that the ocean is much bigger than imagined. Competition for spots on the sports team intensifies and alliances begin to appear. New clothes, haircuts, and hangouts begin to differentiate them from the childish stage which must be left behind.

With awareness of the UGG brand gaining momentum in the surfing market and the mainstream market starting to take notice, angst over making sales became less frequent. Putting in place procedures to cope with the growth, however, now became a greater concern.

The 1985–86 season was a coming-of-age for UGG. Winter cold snaps persisted, the spring Santa Ana conditions arrived late, so reordering was frenzied into February, and we could have booked a quarter-million dollars more in sales if we'd had the product to ship. This was a repeat of the same serious problem we encountered last year, because in Australia, December is midsummer, a season when the nation closes down for the holidays and much of the population takes six-week vacations. Trying to get production rolling during this period had been hopeless. No matter what incentives we threw at Country Leather, the answer was always, "She'll be right, mate! The staff will be back in February and we can fill the orders then." It became obvious that we had to bolster our Christmas inventory to be delivered before they shut down.

But now it was February and our inventory was almost exhausted, so all we could do was tell our customers we were done selling for the season. They weren't done buying, however, so some of them went behind our backs and started calling other factories in Australia to locate an alternative supply of sheepskin boots, which encouraged those manufacturers to expand into the United States and compete with us.

In New Zealand, however, Canterbury Sheepskin was keen to get into the supply chain for UGG. In particular, John Chandler, the shoe designer at Canterbury, was eager to help us. With him, we developed our first style specifically for the ski market.

We knew there was some merit to the resistance to sheepskin boots we'd always encountered from buyers in the ski market: the existing sole on our boots offered little protection from mud and slush, and very little traction on hard-packed snow and ice. John Chandler came up with a new prototype rubber sole for us, and we refined it. At first we called the new design the Slushbuster, later changing the name to Z-Lander as the design was refined.

We were evolving and growing in many ways, and the UGG that showed its wares at ASR in February 1986 was a far different animal from what it had been at the first show. I entered the arena with my head held high, wheeling in the materials for our twenty-foot booth. As we began our setup, a few of the Gordon and Smith sales reps came by to ask if they could carry the UGG line, trying to convince me they could do a great job of taking UGG to the surf market. Inside, I was thinking, *Sure, now that I've built the market and the hard work is done, you want to step in and take easy orders,* but I politely told them I was handling the surf industry myself and did not need any help.

I had come full circle in my understanding of salesmen from the type of people who worked at the used car dealership in Perth. I had learned the big difference between a good salesman who educates, services, and closes versus a mere order taker.

Soon after I began living in California, and while the UGG business was small, I volunteer coached the San Diego State University's rugby team. I asked one of the engineering students what he was going to do after college. "Sales," he said, and I recall being flabbergasted. That was for cash registers and used car lots in my universe. But when he explained that he was being recruited by a company that made large turbine engines, it dawned on me that, of course, they need qualified engineers to understand the product and be able to answer buyers' questions.

At this point in the brand's development, I had come to understand that talking is only a fraction of the sales role, and education, product training, and the art of closing make this a fascinating and rewarding career.

Every part of the exhibition hall was filled, as was an overflow hall just next door.

We had finished putting up our display and were on our way out when—*oh God, no.*

In the most visible position near the entrance, there was Valerie Smith in a booth squeezed up against the wall with her UGHS banner flying high. She had probably had a zillion calls the previous winter because of our undersupply, and now she had discovered the action-sports market. After I had spent six hard, devoted years on the road, developing a formula for surf-shop acceptance, she was ready to cash in on it.

Our booth was in the center of the hall, and it took some time for the buyers to find us. I watched them saunter toward us down the aisle, look up at our UGG logo, and stop dead in their tracks as a perplexed expression came over their faces. You could almost see calculations going on in their heads; then they walked by without making eye contact with us.

Most likely not noticing the difference in spelling of our brand names, many of the buyers stopped at the UGHS booth on the way in and placed orders. Only when they saw our bigger, more professional booth, decked out with enlargements of our ads with pro surfers and a giant UGG logo, did they figure out their mistake.

I seethed all that first day until I realized that all my regular customers were still placing large orders, and we had a lock on most of the biggest stores that were responsible for most of the sheepskin boot sales in California. I consoled myself with the thought that if these new buyers didn't know the difference between authentic UGG brand boots and knockoffs, they must be peripheral retailers who had not been following our advertising.

• • •

Our booth presentation at the ski show in Vegas was another quantum leap in visibility for UGG. Enlarged photos from our ads covered the entire twenty-foot backdrop, and sophisticated lighting made the photos and products stand out. The professional new look gave us greater credibility, and now the major ski-market retailers were coming into the booth to check us out. Paul's sales reps were on hand to meet with their key buyers at the booth, and we saw firsthand the advantage of having a dedicated sales force. Neil was wide-eyed, absorbing his first exposure to the vibrant ski market.

Jamie Walker, the buyer for Sports Chalet—the biggest high-end sporting goods chain in Southern California—came by and asked me to stop by his office the next week to discuss a new order. This was my Holy Grail. I had been trying to get an appointment with him for four years straight.

By the end of April, after my road trips up the coast and the orders coming in from the reps, sales tallied over $600,000, almost as much as our entire year's sales for the previous season, making it at least conceivable that we might hit the million-dollar mark by Christmas.

On the home front, my personal life was evolving as well. My sales commissions for the previous season had totaled more than $30,000. Laura and I were debt-free, and I no longer had to work on Sundays. I had no responsibility for making sure the bills got paid, and didn't have to make dreaded collection calls to slow-paying customers. Neil handled ordering inventory with Country Leather and dealing with George Burcher when there were foul-ups. I was beginning to sense my redundancy at the office, but surprisingly, I wasn't upset. My new life as a "mere" sales rep was turning out to be a lot more fun than running the company.

That summer, while looking for ways to fill my time, I was drawn into the world of Alan Greenway, an Australian businessman who lived in San Diego. A short, wiry man in his sixties, with the typical ruddy face of an Aussie, Alan had started out in the hotel industry with a single motel in a small town called Mudgee (where my father was born) and had parlayed that into owning the Travelodge franchise in Australia. He had served as the head of the Australian Tourism Commission and eventually took over the ownership of Travelodge America, with his office on the downtown waterfront of San Diego Bay.

He had been approached by Ron Tighe, an Australian businessman, to fund a computer business. Alan wanted me to invest with him (and look over Ron's shoulder), so I agreed to put up capital in a 50/50 partnership to help Ron open an office. Alan agreed to float my share until I could pay him back.

After a few months, I realized that Ron was too far behind other software developers to be competitive. I got Alan to agree to pull the plug.

A few months later, when my commission stream from UGG started flowing again, I gave Alan a check for $20,000 for my share of the losses on the computer deal. As we'd had nothing in writing, Alan was surprised to see me again, let alone recoup half of his lost investment.

The simple act of repaying a debt, when others might have seen an opportunity to slip away from a deal gone sour, became the basis of a bond of trust and respect that would prove crucial to UGG several years in the future.

Back on my sales circuit in September, I felt free as a bird. Gone was my anxiety about approaching strangers to ask them to buy something from me. It had been replaced by the pleasure of calling on old friends in the surf shops up and down the coast. Even the owners who had never purchased boots from me before knew me as the UGG guy from my many sales calls, and nearly every store I visited placed an order.

October at last brought a settlement of the UGHS lawsuit with no victory for either side. Valerie Smith hadn't been able to make enough of a case based on the first-use argument to invalidate our UGG trademark, but we didn't want to invest the time and money it would take to invalidate her UGHS trademark. Sticking to my philosophy of "get out in front and run faster," we decided simply to ignore UGHS, knowing we could beat it in the marketplace.

The settlement contained some King Solomon–like baby splitting that was not worth arguing further: UGHS could sell in the United States and emphasize "Made in America," and UGG would continue to sell in the same market, emphasizing our Australian roots.

I sent a copy of the settlement agreement to Neil, Paul Bussmann, and Joe Makalusky, stating that I had now fulfilled my obligation under our contract to buy the business from John Buser and I wanted to exercise my option to get my 25 percent share of stock in UGG. A month later, I received a letter from Joe refusing to let me buy in, based on the fact that the settlement prohibited UGG America, Inc. from using the word *America*.

This made me angry, since the negotiation had been all about marketing and how each brand would be promoted to consumers. The corporate name wouldn't be seen in our advertising anyway, and I felt like this detail was being used as a red herring to prevent me from getting my stock. I seriously doubted that I would ever be an owner of UGG again.

• • •

In the flurry of shipping that followed the arrival of the first winter storms hitting the California coast, a quandary materialized: how many stores within the same area should we sell to? Our faithful early customers who made the gamble of stocking sheepskin boots were protective of their territories and didn't want us to sell UGG products to their competitors who had played it safe until sheepskin boots became popular. We had restricted sales for two seasons even as newcomers clamored to carry our products. But the level of demand from potential new customers was even stronger this year. There was a good argument for leaving the market to sort out, so we decided to set aside our policy and sell to any store that wanted to place an order. The result was something none of us could have predicted.

In the Hermosa Beach area, we had been selling to E.T. Surfboards from the very beginning. We had also opened up Becker's Surf, who came in on the second season. After repeated pleas from Dewey Weber Surf Shop around the corner from E.T., we relented and shipped a small amount of product to them. To everyone's amazement, sales at E.T. and Becker's tripled.

The same phenomena happened with our customers Encinitas Surfboards and Leucadia Surf and Sport. When Julie, the buyer for Hansen's Surf and Sport convinced us to open them, sales tripled for the older customers.

It dawned on us that three stores within a local area passed a tipping point and became some kind of critical mass. In the minds of consumers, the fact that one local store didn't carry UGG brand boots meant that two other stores carrying the product were just coincidences. But if UGG was in every store they went to, it meant this was as essential to surfing as a surfboard.

As we opened up more retailers across the country, we encountered retailers' concern about our selling to their nearby competitors time after time, but we forged ahead anyway, knowing that the critical-mass effect would favor everyone. The rising tide of the UGG phenomenon was lifting all retailers to higher levels of sales and profits.

• • •

Nineteen eighty-six marked the year of our entrance into the malls. Impressed by the huge number of moms looking for UGG brand boots during the previous season, Kinney's and Thom McAn stepped up to buy inventory. But here again, retailers' fear of having too much product available on their turf became an issue.

Dave Nash, the owner of a chain of surf wear shops called Sun Diego, was taking surf fashion into the mall locations, and Sun Diego contacted me with a big order. Most of the hard-core surf shop owners were up in arms about that, seeing the arrival of a "mall surf shop" as a rip-off by stores "who don't even make their own surfboards!" We tested the waters by supplying Sun Diego with a small inventory of UGG brand boots. Overall demand was so strong that all surf shops in California nearly doubled their sales and the Sun Diego crisis was over before it really began.

By November, due to the high volume of telephone reorders, I was of more value helping out in the warehouse at Anaheim than I was on the road managing inventories. It was a daily challenge to keep up with the orders, made more challenging when it became apparent our until-then-unproven new Z-Lander line was flying out retailers' doors.

Around this time, an old friend from my Perth accounting days sent me an article from an Australian business magazine that told the story of Country Leather and how they had "cracked the US market." As I read, I kept anticipating the part where my role in their success would be covered. If I'd blinked, I would have missed it—George Burcher simply mentioned "a contact in America." I had to laugh. George had made a handsome profit supplying sheepskin boots to me for the past six years, while I'd been suffering five years of losses along the lonesome shop-by-shop sales road, building the sheepskin footwear business into a credible category. I knew our sales in America were soon to outpace George's capacity to supply us, and once again I had a sense of dread when I thought of our longtime partnership.

I'm sure that in George's mind it really was him building a thriving export business in Australia. I wasn't threatened by that. My sense of dread was around the fact that he was oblivious to the buying power of the American market, and how he might react when he realized he was just a small part of the supply chain that I knew was building, as I added distribution channels across the country.

• • •

The Christmas rush was frantic. Our shipping staff was run ragged, so for two weeks I pitched in to help, unloading, sorting, and labeling incoming boots, and watching them being pulled for shipment as fast as I could put them into inventory. The local retailers couldn't wait the extra day for UPS delivery, so they arrived at the warehouse two and three times a week to grab whatever was available.

After Christmas, we ran the year's tally. We had done it! UGG had cracked the million-dollar barrier. We broke out the beer and toasted a whopping $1.4 million in sales! All it had taken was seven long years of pounding the pavement, painful belt-tightening during the many times we were broke, countless sleepless nights, and relentless dreaming.

In the calm before the new year, I reflected on my life and goals. Every entrepreneur dreams of building a million-dollar business, and I had done it. Although I was not an owner, it did not diminish the satisfaction I felt in creating a youthful business that still had huge potential.

We were still primarily a California business, with most of our sales in a tiny niche of surfing, and a million dollars seemed so trivial compared to my visions of what UGG could be. We had built credibility in the local footwear retail industry, withstood the attacks of a hostile competitor, evolved a quality product that we were proud to sell, and had staff and financing in place to keep growing.

At home, Laura and I were financially comfortable, and I saw a future of increasing commissions for work that I considered fun, and few summer duties, which left lots of time for vacations, surfing, and golf. And, to top things off, we had recently heard the heartbeat of our first child, Erika.

I was living the American dream!

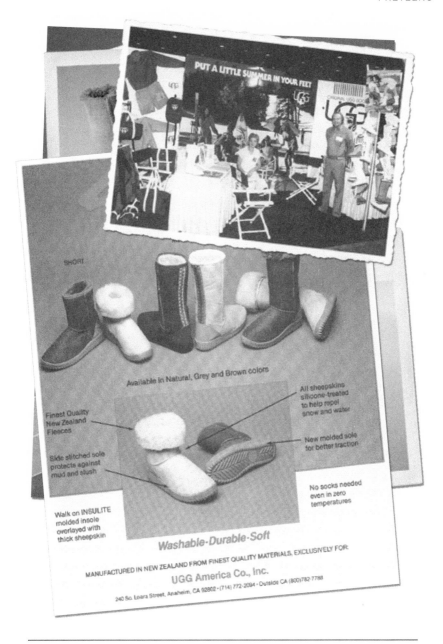

Top: Neil Fearing and Maria Bussmann at the ski show booth with hanging display.
Bottom: Z-Lander boot.

CHAPTER 7

TWEENS

The Calm before the Storm
1987—Sales $2 million

Junior high school can be both exciting and agonizing for a youth, a roller coaster of strength and confidence one moment, vulnerability and anxiety the next. As parents can attest, it's no easier on them. With luck, mutually beneficial relationships deepen into something else: mutual respect.

Nineteen eighty-seven was by far the easiest for me, a year that would prove to be the calm before the storm.

January started off brilliantly. During the Christmas rush, there were several competing brands of sheepskin boots on sale in all sorts of retail stores. I was worried that, because of our poor delivery in the previous season, the popularity of the UGG brand would be smothered by the wave of newcomers. But then retailers began calling us, saying, "Can we place an order for UGG? We tried products from a different vendor, but our customers keep returning them. They tell us they just want the UGG brand."

We eventually figured out that, in November and December, kids were telling their parents they wanted UGG sheepskin boots for Christmas. Moms who didn't know the difference were buying competitors' sheepskin boots. Then after Christmas, the kids were refusing to wear them because the cool people at school made fun of them for wearing "fake UGG boots." We even had consumers calling our office to ask if they could swap competitors' boots for real UGG brand boots, because the retailers wouldn't refund their money.

Perception is everything. The UGG brand had gradually assumed a powerful image. As the year of 1987 dawned, I felt I was on Easy Street at last. I had no office duties, and my commission checks kept rolling in. Life was good!

But my disillusionment grew about the fading likelihood of ever getting my stock in UGG America, Inc. Joe Makalusky was becoming more combative every time I raised the issue, and Paul and Neil gave me little support. The full significance of relinquishing control of the company by selling more than 51 percent of the business began to dawn on me. I was troubled by a growing awareness that I no longer controlled my own destiny. What if I got fired?

I was dependent on my income from being a sales rep, so without telling Neil, Paul, or Joe, I enrolled in a real estate course to become a licensed business broker, hoping to equip myself with a fallback career that would serve me in the event I decided to leave UGG.

In the meantime, to show Paul that I was still earning my keep, I went on the road again, to stores and trade shows. As I studied my sales printout to see how much each store had bought the previous season, it began to dawn on me that their UGG profits were paying a significant part of each store's annual wages and overhead. That abject fear of selling that I had been overcoming for five years was almost gone, and now I felt like a benefactor every time I revisited a store.

At the Long Beach and Atlantic City trade shows, buyers were placing good orders in February because they were confident of strong sell-through next season. Finally, the East Coast attitude that sheepskin boots were just a fad was evaporating, and for the first time, were ordering with staggered delivery dates so they wouldn't be left scrambling for fill-ins at the height of the season.

At the ski show in March, we set up our familiar surf-ski backdrop and Misty Sprinkle's Hawaiian Tropic girls kept the tall white boots in high visibility throughout the show, while Paul Bussmann's sales reps worked with a steady stream of buyers. Thinking back to our original Six-Pair Stocking Plan, I was astonished to realize that our typical order was now close to sixty pairs.

After the trade shows, I traveled the country from Seattle to New Jersey, working with the reps on their sales techniques. None of them, I was horrified to discover, were asking the buyers to try on the boots in their bare feet. The most common objection was, "We always wear socks. This isn't California!"

However, after two or three sales calls, each rep began to see the power of the "Oh my God" reaction from every buyer who felt sheepskin fleece on their bare feet and ankles, and sales soared.

From the retailers from Chicago to New York, the common question was, "Are they waterproof?" Every store had two types of waterproof boots: the heavy, rubber, Sorel type for mud and slush, and the sleek, fashionable mid-calf boots made from treated waterproof Napa leather, lined with synthetic fleece. In the buyers' minds, they already had the category covered, from heavy, ugly, practical boots to fashion-conscious (but freezing cold) high-heeled styles. According to their reports, the bulky, unstructured sheepskin boots looked totally inadequate to the average shopper. I knew we had some serious work to do on product development if we were to crack the Midwest and Eastern markets in a big way.

The other thing I noticed was that few people East of the Rockies were even aware of the UGG brand. Nobody in Minneapolis, New York, Chicago, or Indianapolis read *Surfer* or *Surfing* magazine. Eastern consumers were more likely to snow ski, but our ski-oriented advertising had been restricted to trade publications. On the flight back to California, I mulled over the image we needed to present in the mainstream media in order to make UGG a sought-after item. I recalled how instantly successful our professional surfer ads had been in California—what would make Midwesterners want to "jump into our ads"?

May 1987 was a cruise for me, since the surf-shop owners were preparing for summer sales and didn't need to see me. My commission checks for the prior season had exceeded $60,000. The Pacific Beach area had grown into a rowdy singles scene, so we purchased a new home in Leucadia, about thirty-five miles north where the suburban lifestyle seemed more appropriate for parents of a new baby. Best of all, the location cut about forty-five minutes off my increasingly intolerable commute to the warehouse. I was surfing a lot, playing golf, and generally enjoying my newfound freedom from running the business.

I spent quite a bit of time in the Anaheim warehouse helping Neil process orders from the shows and the reps. Joe Makalusky, whose job from the outset was to handle the accounting, was proving unreliable. He never brought the urgently needed computer system completely online, a serious problem as just our pre-season sales were approaching the entire previous year's total. We were looking at a potential two-million-dollar year.

• • •

With time on my hands, I took a brief trip back to Australia, making a stop in Sydney to meet with the owners of Scaffa Boots, who were interested in being a supplier to UGG America. I didn't commit, but I couldn't shake the feeling that something bad was going to happen with George and Country Leather, so I made a note to keep Scaffa in mind.

As fall 1987 came around, I again worked in the warehouse to unload the containers arriving from Country Leather. By now, George Burcher had enough faith in us—at least while Neil's letters of credit came on time—to begin manufacturing boots in advance and sending them by ocean to arrive in September and each month thereafter. My routine was to count, organize by style and size, label, and restock the boots into the racking system for later pulling. Neil Fearing and I bonded during these days at the office, and he admitted that he'd come to appreciate how much work it had taken to establish UGG in the years before he bought in.

He told me that when surf shop owners called in, they always asked about me and said good things about me. I was flattered, but pointed out it was simply my way of doing business: my road trips and my style of over-the-top customer service had paid off in valuable brand loyalty.

Neil was also impressed that, despite being a non-owner of the business, I had yielded gracefully to perform my job on the road, and I always came in to help out in panic-mode shipping crises. He saw that my obsession with growing the company and the UGG brand took precedence over ego or personal gain.

This may be the reason that, one day in October, he unexpectedly announced, "We need to get new company cars!"

While my customer service to the retailers was designed to create more sales and loyalty, my service in the warehouse was an unconscious act of helping the team through tough periods. I certainly wasn't sucking up to Neil for brownie points, but it was pleasing for me to watch his attitude changing, even to the point where he recognized me as more of a team member than Joe, and this unconscious helping out would come full circle for me next year when Neil overrode Joe's objections and began the process of issuing my shares. There is a Universal law wherein every act of giving has to go full circle to complete its karmic journey.

I had been battling the road in my old Audi that had 140,000 miles on it and was thinking of replacing it with a new Audi or a BMW. Neil suggested I go down to the new Acura dealership. I'd never heard of Acura, but I fell in love with the first car I test drove, and within days, Neil signed the company to a lease.

Feeling flush, I laid out $1,200 for one of the first mobile phones to install in my new car, to make my road trips more efficient. At last I was free of gas station phones and their tattered yellow pages!

I did the rounds of the surf shops in Southern California that fall in the new car, and in the bigger stores, I put on a series of clinics to teach the sales staffs about the importance of having their customers try the boots on without socks.

Back in Anaheim, while helping with the pre-Christmas shipping, I noticed that sales of women's sizes were beginning to catch up with the men's. Now schoolgirls had decided UGG was a hot item, and even the moms were beginning to buy a pair for themselves when they bought for the kids. Once again, stores dispatched their delivery trucks to our warehouse to pick up stock so they wouldn't lose a day with UPS.

Our ads in *Action Sports* and *Outdoor* magazines were driving the retailers, and the ads in *Surfer*, *Surfing*, and now *Powder* were driving the consumers. I had come to know a fellow surfer, Shawn Styles, who was doing the Surf Report on the local radio station. He mentioned he needed a sponsor for the San Diego market. We agreed to a nominal fee, and soon, every morning, Shawn was blasting out over the radio, "This is the surf report brought to you by UGG. The surf is . . . the water temperature is . . . and it's a good day for UGG brand boots!"

To get a feel for what was happening on the retail scene, I did a quick road trip up the coast. When I stopped in at Newport Surf and Sport, I was shocked to find that they had imported seventy cartons of Scaffa Boots from Australia. This was a serious competitive threat, especially since the store owner told me he intended to resell these boots to other surf retailers. Here was our first competitor who had the ability to inventory boots and handle reorders, which I knew to be the key to sustaining business. I chided myself for not being in a financial position to let Scaffa be a supplier when I met with them in Australia, back in June.

Every entrepreneur starting out is concerned that their idea will be copied and imitated in the marketplace. If you provide a good product or service, and it does well in the marketplace, then it is almost guaranteed that there will be knockoffs. The secret to sustaining your leadership is to always strive for innovation that keeps you one step ahead of the imitators. The greatest asset that you have is vision. *You see what is possible, but the imitators just see what you have done.*

• • •

Busier than ever, Neil Fearing was getting out of shape; even though he looked fine and carried no extra weight for his small stature, he wasn't physically fit. More than once I noticed him sit down to catch his breath after lifting cartons up into the racks. At the warehouse, I would often find him out of breath, sitting at the top of the stairs. I'd joke with him about joining a health club to get in shape, but he never seemed seriously interested.

He and I were getting along great now, and he confided in me that there was conflict among Joe Makalusky, Paul Bussmann, and himself. I surmised that the terms of their agreement to equally fund the business hadn't panned out, and now Neil was carrying the burden of the financing. Neil agreed that I had lived up to my end of the deal by settling the UGHS lawsuit, though Joe was still a holdout on the issue. Neil asked me if I was ready to buy in to the company. I said I'd been ready for a long time. He thought about it for a moment, then told me he'd put together the legal documents to make it happen.

Between Christmas and New Year's, we performed our annual ritual of going through the books for the year. When Neil hit the "Total Sales" button, a cheer went up. We had broken the two-million-dollar barrier!

It seemed that everything had fallen into place in the past twelve months. I was enjoying my work and getting paid really well to do it. The brand was becoming well-known and the product didn't need to be explained anymore in California. Good financing made it seem too easy to increase sales by almost a million dollars. Yes, this was why I got into the business in the first place.

Top: Hawaiian Tropic girls. *Bottom, from left to right*: Paul Bussmann, Della Fearing, Laura Smith, Jim Whittaker, Maria Bussmann, Bob and Carol London, Doug Price, Brian, and George Burcher at ski show booth.

CHAPTER 8

PUBERTY

Reversal of Fortune
1988—Sales $1.6 million

Few of us make it to maturity without at least one devastating heartbreak or setback. Even significant success can suddenly give way to the genuine possibility of failure due to a single unforeseen event beyond anyone's control.

The first part of 1988 started off nicely. Neil Fearing and I signed the documents for my buy-in of 25 percent of UGG America, Inc., and I transferred the trademark. Neil also bought out Paul Bussmann and Joe Makalusky, retaining Paul as sales manager. I was now fully addicted to the regular commission checks I'd been getting, and expected to receive close to $100,000 over the next few months. But with the new ownership arrangement, administrative details now fell back to me, and my life was about to get busier.

My first order of business was to "get out front and run faster." Since competitors were copying our styles and colors, we changed our Cinnamon to Sand and for the first time decided to try black, as well as a gray shade we named Charcoal.

My commission checks were exceeding $20,000 per month, and since the warehouse staff had the January shipping under control, Laura and I decided to do a quick trip to Australia to show off our daughter to the family. For the first time in ten years, we felt optimism and freedom from bills. It was such a relief to take my eyes off the business for a few days and enjoy the benefits of the financial freedom that had always been our goal.

Making a routine visit to the warehouse after my return, I found Neil sitting at the top of the stairs near his office. The warehouse manager, Neil's longtime friend Bob London, took me aside and told me that he had been with Neil at a motocross race the previous weekend. An avid cyclist, Neil had just completed a race when Bob found him sitting on the ground near his van with his bike on its side, half-hoisted into the van. Neil had told Bob he didn't have the energy to get it all the way in.

A week later Neil said to me, "We need to get some life insurance."

He called up one of his friends who sold insurance for Transamerica, and we filled out the forms. I got my physical exam; Neil didn't. I recall thinking it was strange that only Neil and I were doing this. Why not Paul and Joe as well?

• • •

To my surprise, while I'd been in Australia, Neil had purchased fifteen hundred pairs of boots from a competitor, Greg Johnson. Greg was one of those retailers who couldn't sell the knockoff boots he'd purchased from a supplier and tagged with his own brand name, Outback Boots. Neil acquired Greg's remaining stock for about one-quarter of what Country Leather charged us for our boots. Their quality was decent, and Neil already had a buyer in the closeout business to take them off our hands.

One Saturday in late February, I rented a truck and drove to Greg's warehouse in Vista, just north of San Diego. I had always resented others coming into "my" sheepskin boot market and prepared myself not to like him, but we hit it off immediately. I packed the boots into the truck and drove to Anaheim, spending the rest of the day sorting them out in the warehouse.

Around sunset, as I was driving home through San Clemente, a call came in on my new car phone. Laura was crying.

Neil had died.

He had been in a motocross race and suffered a massive heart attack. He was pronounced dead when he arrived at the hospital.

For a few minutes, my mind went numb, until I began to put two and two together. *He knew*, I thought. All those times I chided him to join a health club flashed back to me, and I recalled how he had just laughed. Was this why he bought the insurance policies? Was he expecting to die soon? Did he keep his worries to himself to avoid jeopardizing the insurance?

Maybe I should have been thinking of Neil's family or contemplating the fickleness of life; however, from the center of my universe, the thoughts that ran through my head in those first few minutes were: *What's the effect of this on Laura and me? What does this mean for my royalty checks? What's the status of the buyout arrangement with Paul and Joe?*

I consoled Laura and began to make calls. I spoke with Neil's wife, Della, and arranged to meet with her early Monday morning. I called Paul and then made the call to George Burcher, who was devastated. He had dealt with uncertainty for five years with me, and no sooner had his payment stream become reliable than it was up in the air again. I asked him to send me a list of invoices that had not been paid and assured him I would look into them the following week.

That night in bed, a chill came over me, perhaps the opposite of the goose bumps that always alerted me to a brilliant opportunity. This time it was a sense of foreboding, a certainty that I would soon be facing something terrible and it was time to hunker down and be strong and smart.

When I met Della at the warehouse, it was obvious she had little knowledge of Neil's business affairs, so I committed to do everything in my power to keep the operation running as usual until we sorted out where the company stood financially. I surmised, and Della confirmed, that Neil had been personally funding operations, and that his estate would consist largely of assets tied up in UGG. Della and I were left as co-owners of UGG America, Inc., subject to my sorting out where the process of the buyout of Paul and Joe stood. Together, Della and I called a staff meeting, and we asked them all to carry on, as Neil would have wanted.

Things flow smoothly in crisis times, such as the death of a key stakeholder, if the founders have planned for this when beginning the company or by changing the ownership structure as it matures. It is common to have a buyout mechanism in place for the survivors to follow, and often there are insurance policies in place to provide the cash. Often the last thing you want is to be running the company with your ex-partner's heirs trying to call the shots.

Thank God we had inventory and there were a few shipments still on their way from Australia. We were able to keep shipping to our customers without interruption and keep the cash flow coming in.

The ski industries show, just a week away in March, now became a priority, so after Paul and his wife, Maria, came out for Neil's funeral, we all set off for Las Vegas.

Aside from the Hawaiian Tropic girls parading around in UGG, the highlight of this show was when Jim Whittaker arrived at the booth. Jim, the first American to summit Mount Everest, had learned about UGG from his nephew's visit to our booth two years before.

An imposing figure at least six and a half feet tall with weathered skin and a rugged, almost gaunt face, a disarming smile, and a pair of piercing but friendly eyes, Jim explained that he was in the planning stages of an international expedition. His goal was to have climbers from America, Russia, and China all reach the summit of Mount Everest on Earth Day 20, April 22, 1990. He called it the Peace Climb.

We signed on as a potential sponsor and sent a box of boots for him and his organizers to field-test in the mountains. Convincing him to try on the boots without socks was a challenge—this was the type of guy who probably wore socks to bed—but a month later he called just raving about wearing the boots sockless in twenty-below-zero temperatures for hours on end, while his feet stayed at body temperature the whole time. Although we knew that sheepskin has the best insulating properties of any product available, Jim's firsthand experience gave us new credibility, and we lost no time in asking if we could quote him. His endorsement featured prominently in our next round of promotional material.

Then began the most physically demanding nine months of my life. I found myself commuting more than four hours every day to and from the warehouse, and life became a blur of fourteen-hour days. I began taking the train to Anaheim on Monday mornings; Laura picked me up in Del Mar late on Fridays. I came to despise the cheesy brown décor of the rooms at the Disneyland Sheraton, the closest hotel to the warehouse, and I became a regular diner at the Bob's Big Boy down the block. Apart from yoga stretches in my hotel room, exercise took a backseat.

I was run-down at the end of every week, nursing a chronic sore throat. Even on the brink of being bedridden, I somehow I managed to propel myself back to work every Monday. I was weary to my core, and sleep was fitful because of the many unknowns spinning around in my head.

After the Ski Show, Paul came to the warehouse to help sort things out. As if we'd opened Pandora's box, surprises were common and we had to make decisions very fast.

We were appalled at the stacks of orders in Neil's filing system that should have been shipped weeks earlier. Then Paul found a drawer that contained thousands of dollars of uncashed COD checks, some months old. When we tried to run sales reports from the computer, nothing reconciled. We had no idea what had been invoiced, which accounts had paid, and which accounts owed us money. Sales totals were wrong and nothing linked to the general ledger. We would have to re-create the entire year's sales, entry by entry, from the shipping invoices and the sales deposit slips.

While Paul got busy on the shipping details, I decided to hire an auditor, study the computer system, check the buyout documents, and keep Country Leather happy. I also made a call to Carl Brown, my patent attorney. The first question he asked was, "Are the royalties up-to-date?" Now that he mentioned it, I realized I hadn't seen a royalty check to UGG Imports for use of the trademark for the whole year, so he insisted that I write a notice of default letter to UGG America, Inc. This took some effort on Carl's part to convince me, as I didn't want to appear to be attacking the company at the same time I claimed to be trying to help save it.

I was suddenly faced with a huge moral dilemma. I had spent years in Australia as public accountant, specializing in winding up insolvent companies, so I knew the legal ramifications of asset distribution. I knew that UGG America was delinquent in paying the royalties back to UGG Imports and that I could have attempted to take the trademark back by default and start again. But, on the other hand, Della had no idea what was going on inside the company, and I felt an obligation to salvage the best possible solution for her, as I thought Neil would have done for Laura in different circumstances. I decided to hang in there and keep UGG America alive (and send the default letter as insurance in case things were unsalvageable).

Then I received a letter from Joe Makalusky declaring that, since his buyout was never signed, he and Paul were now the rightful owners of UGG America, Inc. I spoke with Della and her lawyers. They pointed out that the buyout agreement required Joe and Paul to come forward with considerable funds. Were Joe and Paul prepared to fulfill their obligation with cash payments at this time? Apparently not, because Joe never replied. This challenge, at least, was quickly averted.

I studied Neil's life insurance policy and called the agent, who told me there was no way the policy would pay out, since Neil had never completed his medical checkup. So next thing, I called an insurance attorney friend, Maynard Kartvedt. He drafted a letter to make a claim, and I sent this off to Transamerica Life with little expectation of success.

When I pulled out the file of Country Leather purchases and began wading through the customs brokers' delivery invoices, I calculated that we owed Country Leather $76,000. I called George Burcher to confirm this figure.

George was in a panic. He wasn't aware that I had come back into the business and had been calling Della (who knew nothing), Bob London (who knew nothing), and Neil's accountant (who knew nothing). When I called, he realized that I was his only hope of finding a savior. He explained that he was pressed financially and owed a lot of money to his suppliers of raw sheepskin. He'd be out of business within weeks if we didn't pay what we owed him.

For my part, I knew that our future was riding on the back of Country Leather; we'd be begging George for credit if we were going to ship anything next season.

I delivered Greg Johnson's Outback Boots to the closeout buyer, collected a check for $37,500 and, together with the cash from the COD checks Paul had found in Neil's drawer, sent George two-thirds of what we owed, praying he would remember my gesture of good faith.

• • •

For the entire month of April, I was a forensic accountant, working backward through the files and two years of bank statements to reconcile income transactions. None of this matched up with sales invoices and Neil's computer printouts were so convoluted that I finally threw my hands up in despair and told Lisa, our bookkeeper, to purge the entire computer. Together, we zeroed out every account, and then she entered the actual sales we had delivered for the past twelve months by looking at every shipped invoice.

"I don't give a damn about what colors, styles, or numbers of boots went out," I told her, "just give me the invoice number and the total."

Each Friday as my commuter train pulled out of Anaheim, I compared the stack of invoices with the printout from the computer, made corrections, and packed up the paperwork as the train pulled into Del Mar. I did my best to hide that I didn't feel well as our one-year-old, Erika, jumped into my arms and Laura drove us home. I think I slept straight through every Saturday for probably six months, fitting in some family time around midday on Sundays.

In early May, when we had almost finished with the order entry, Lisa called me and said, "The computer just crashed."

"Okay," I replied calmly. "Let's just go back to the last time you backed up and continue from there."

"Backed up?" she said.

"Oh God . . . Just start from the first invoice and let's do it all again."

My chartered accountant's sixth sense was tingling, and I got the feeling that the outcome was not going to be good. My instincts told me to expect about a $90,000 shortfall. I called Bob London, our former warehouse manager and Neil's close friend, to seek his advice about how to break this to Della.

It was then that Bob told me what everyone was thinking. There was a lot of bad feeling about how I was running the business. It was perceived, among other things, that I had hired auditors and a lawyer without consulting with Della, that Paul and I had a secret scheme cooking to steal the business, that I was going to sue Della if she didn't sell out everything to me, and that I had fired Bob without telling her.

Bob's words hit me like a bomb. I was horrified that I had been so insensitive to the people around me that they could so wildly misinterpret why I'd been knocking myself out all these weeks.

Fear of the unknown leads to paranoia. My own fear of not knowing where the company stood had my head down for fourteen hours a day trying to make some sense of the accounting and legal issues. I was so self-absorbed that I was not aware that my lack of communication with the others was feeding their own fears. Honest communication always brings enlightenment, and from this episode I learned to keep key people in the loop, especially if things were not looking good.

While all this was going on, I felt I had to keep up the appearance to outsiders that UGG was functioning normally. Paul's sales force was kicking into high gear, and the new orders coming in were about to overtake the $330,000 we wrote at the Ski Show. Dana Hatch, a sales rep from the action-sports industry, came on board to service the surf market that had been my responsibility. Blond, bubbly, and intelligent, Dana already knew most of our retailers, so she was a good fit to take over my own road trips.

Maynard Kartvedt, the insurance attorney, called to report he had received a letter from Transamerica Life denying the claim on Neil's policy. He told me, "Don't worry. They always reject claims as a first step to test whether you're willing to give up without a fight. I'll follow up to let them know we're going to fight."

We were still shipping sporadic orders, and our sizes were running out, so I faxed an order to George. His faxed reply had an icy, legalistic tone uncharacteristic of the George I knew: "It would be irresponsible for me to send more boots with the state of affairs as they are now."

Although I agreed with him, I had a shiver of suspicion that this might be the first shot across our bow to let me know he was contemplating cutting us off.

Then I received a surprising call from the new owner of UGHS, Peter Raffin, who told me he had let Valerie go and asked me if I was interested in buying his business. My mouth salivated at the prospect—what a delicious proposition, to finally prevail over Valerie Smith—but it was ludicrous to act on this at the same time UGG was floundering. I told him I'd think about it and speak with my partners, and that's where I left the matter. In reality, it would be many months before we were able to even discuss the idea again.

• • •

Late in May 1987, some morning at 1:30 AM, I made the final keystroke on the calculator to see a loss of $79,000. UGG America was doomed.

I was exhausted, but I made the long drive home to Leucadia and fell into bed around 3:30 AM. Along the way, my mind was a blizzard of anxieties. *Should I give up? UGG is insolvent! I hate working in Anaheim! No one except me knows all the intricacies of running the business. Do I owe it to Della to keep working like this when I own only 25 percent of the business? Will UGG ever be profitable?*

I was run-down, fighting the ongoing throat issue, feeling like antibiotics were the only thing keeping me going apart from my family. I talked with Laura about the options, knowing there was no way I was going to get a regular job in accounting. We discussed other business opportunities, but none came close to the promise of UGG if it could be properly financed.

Preseason orders were so strong that we were looking at a three-million-dollar sales season. It would be a crime to let such promise go down the drain. On the other hand, with no money, UGG was on track to crash and burn into ashes, and Della and I would end up with nothing.

I called Alan Greenway to get his advice. He asked me to prepare a business plan, a hint that he might step in with financing. This glimmer of hope was the log in the rapids I clung to. I called Della and told her the only way I was willing to carry on—and realistically, the only way for her to get any value for Neil's assets tied up in the company—was for me to buy her out completely.

Paul Bussmann called and read to me a scathing letter that Della's lawyer had faxed to Della, Joe, and him, warning them to "protect themselves from Brian Smith . . . He's trying to steal the business and will revoke the trademark." I asked Paul to set up a meeting with Della and her lawyer for the next day.

At Della's attorney's office, the mood was more realistic. Della had resigned herself to the fact that, even if she kept the business, she didn't have a clue what to do with it. She and her lawyer realized that I was their best hope of liquidating the remaining inventory and cutting the ongoing overheads. There was really nothing to talk about. She agreed to the buyout.

On my drive home to Leucadia, for the first time in months I felt energized and inspired. UGG had another chance! I still had hundreds of loyal customers, and I was determined not to let them down.

To start, I asked Paul what his intentions were concerning the sales force. He told me that he and his wife had been contemplating a move to California and were interested in working full-time for UGG.

Working down my list, I crossed off the purchase of UGHS as impractical and honed in on "hire a computer programmer." I called Conrad Mouton, a close friend I had known since 1979 when we had volunteer coached San Diego State University's rugby team. He was now a computer programmer.

We met at Conrad's ceiling fan business. I described the mess I was in, the brand's brilliant possibilities and its immediate challenges, the tangle of the accounting system we'd inherited from Neil, the deadlines hanging over me, the legal entanglements, my debts of honor to Neil's widow and the company's employees, and my commitments as a husband and father.

He listened to it all and, miraculously, was enthusiastic about our future and surprisingly willing to abandon his ceiling fan business. He agreed, as a first step, to create the Excel spreadsheets I desperately needed for a business plan to court investors.

In the next few days, without waiting for a contract or even the likelihood of getting paid, Conrad created a program for order entry that assured we could input all of the orders received for shipping in the fall.

Our health had progressed from "life support" to merely "critical."

As dire as the internal workings of the company were, there were a lot of positive things happening on the outside. The sales reps had been extremely successful in bringing in orders for the fall, and no one outside of our small group had any idea that the company was on the brink of disaster. The best thing was that at last I knew where the company stood, even if it was not pretty. I harbored a secret optimism that Maynard would be successful in getting an insurance settlement and the thought of having competent accounting and office management with Conrad, Paul, and Maria was especially reassuring.

I was beginning to formulate a plan to buy Della out and believed that, if I could own the company again, I would be able to find investors to bankroll the purchase of inventory and save the day.

Ahh, the thrill of being an entrepreneur!

Jim Whittaker and Brian at Las Vegas ski show.

CHAPTER 9

EARLY TEENS

Back in Business—Again
1988 continued—Sales $1.6 Million

Graduation from junior high school and entering into high school signals a major step toward maturity for a young person and powerful new challenges for a parent. A child's achievements abruptly lose their significance in the face of broader competition. Supportive teachers are replaced with sometimes arbitrary, demanding authority figures. It's also a time when the best-friends-forever relationships of childhood have a tendency to end, fading gently or exploding in "I'm never going to talk to you again!" This same major step is necessary for a business, when past relationships become tenuous and future growth requires new partners and strategies.

It was now June. We had orders for about $1.5 million on the books and no way to supply any of it.

I set Paul to work on the rebate forms for the Australian Export Development program, and he found $57,000 that was eligible. We sent the paperwork off to George for him to get the rebate and give us credit for future purchases.

We finally finished the business plan. I delivered a copy to Alan Greenway; he said that he was interested in discussing it further, but only if he and his partner had control.

And then, the universe stepped in. I received a call from Steve Nitzberg, who asked if he could help with financing. A tall, fit man with graying hair and a friendly disposition, Steve explained that he was a consultant specializing in businesses that served the action-sports market. We spent a couple of hours discussing the state of UGG.

"Whatever you do, don't give up control," he emphasized, "You have $1.5 million in potential receivables, and I can help you find a factor to finance your sales."

Factoring companies will pay you 80 percent of invoices after the product has been shipped. The factor takes direct ownership of the invoices, does the collecting, and makes its money on a commission on what it collects. You get the remaining 20 percent (less commissions) when the customer pays.

For a business that has consistent year-round sales, factoring can be a great method of obtaining cash to run the ongoing operations. It is usually an option for newer businesses that are still too risky for a traditional bank to supply a line of credit at low rates, and the penalty is that factors are quite a bit more expensive to borrow from. Another downside is, because of the extra risk, the factoring companies will usually require that the business sign over all its assets as security for all the monies they advance against invoices. In a consistent business, this is not a big deal, but I was to learn that for UGG, who had a frantic three months of shipping and overheads, but a history of slow-paying customers from the ski industry, our lack of ongoing invoices caused the cash advances to dry up before we could pay back all the draws.

The prospect of having cash now rather than sweating out each invoice seemed like a godsend, so we immediately retained Steve to begin the process. I was desperate for any bit of good news I could pass along to George, so I called to tell him about my progress in being able to pay him and did my best to encourage him to stay in the game.

There was also bad news. Dana Hatch called to say she'd heard from several of our surf-shop accounts that they had been approached by a company called Thunderwear that was trying to get orders for sheepskin boots they were calling THUGGS. I had never heard of Thunderwear, so I thumbed through issues of *Action Sports* until I found an ad for their nylon gloves and accessories; apparently, Thunderwear was targeting the new sport of windsurfing. *Why are they doing sheepskin?* I asked myself. *And where are they getting the boots?* It was disturbing that they were sailing so close to our trademark.

When Paul stepped in with the news that he'd just received an order from L.L. Bean for 816 pairs of Tall, Sand color boots, I put the Thunderwear matter out of my mind. L.L. Bean was very good news indeed. We had been trying for several years to get them to place their first order with us. Now, at last, it had come.

Although the order itself would be profitable, by far the most valuable part of the deal for us would be the exposure. The company's reputation for selling only the highest-quality products meant an implicit validation of our products' quality. Millions of new consumers across the country would become aware of UGG through the company's catalog customers.

Getting retail exposure in the best shoe stores was always on my mind for the same reason. Since we already had a fantastic presence in Sports Chalet, which was the pinnacle of California sporting good stores, my new Holy Grail was Nordstrom, for the supreme validation of our brand.

Although printed catalogs still persist, they are a fraction of the volume before the internet. Shopping on cell phones or computers is so fast and sophisticated now, with the retailer being able to change styles and selling prices at will and even giving up-to-the-second availability of every item. Our L.L. Bean sale would be the equivalent of getting your product into an online store like Zappos.

I had been sending orders to Country Leather as fast as we were writing the business, but George was becoming evasive as to whether or not he was going to ship to me. I assumed he was making product, since I was in contact with some of the tanned-skin suppliers and knew he had been purchasing a lot of skins in our new colors of black and charcoal. None of the other competitors had these colors in their line, so it seemed logical that George was going to wait until I could confirm payment prior to shipping me the boots he was stockpiling.

However, since the months were passing and I was worried that George's deliveries might not be sufficient for our first shipments, as insurance, I was also in contact with Doug Price at Canterbury Sheepskins in New Zealand. Doug said that he had the capacity to make six thousand pairs of boots with a six-week delivery date, and that he was coming to San Diego to talk with me about financing. Time was getting tight—it was now July, and we knew customers would be wanting their boots beginning in mid-August.

• • •

I'd gone from being the contented salesman out on the road to wearing every hat in managing and operating the company, in a desperate effort to make things appear as normal as possible to our customers. We booked ads in *Action Sports, Surfer,* and *Surfing* magazines, and ordered two ads in *Powder* magazine for the November and December issues. We would have to come up with the money to pay for them soon after the ads ran.

Also on my mind: I still hadn't completed the deal to buy out Della.

While Steve Nitzberg was on the road looking for factors, I began shopping the business plan around. Every bank I visited told me, "You're crazy . . . sheepskin boots are a fad. You guys won't be around for long. Thanks, but no."

I called Randy, my rugby buddy in the Chicago finance world. Again, he said, "I'm still not sure sheepskin boots will ever catch on. No thanks."

Although Alan Greenway wouldn't budge on wanting control, he did talk to an associate of his who worked at Nike. I was surprised to learn from Alan that the guy at Nike had said he and his marketing director had been watching the growth of UGG for two years. They had pretty much decided we were too small for them, but I felt pleased that UGG was even on Nike's radar!

I was playing a weak hand, trying to keep my game face on for the outside world while knowing I didn't have a solid solution for supplying our customers. The uncertainty of the situation was wearing me down.

I was surfing at Beacons Beach when I saw Butch Barr out in the water. Butch was one of the founders of Rip Curl, a force within the surfing community based out of Torquay in Australia. After our wave session, I approached him in the parking lot. Soon we were talking about my predicament. Butch was very sympathetic, telling me that his company had faced nearly identical growth issues. Hearing him say that, knowing his enterprise had pulled through, did a lot in the next weeks to keep me positive and forging ahead in my efforts to refinance. As we parted, he told me, "No matter what, don't give up control."

My experience of losing control of the business when I teamed with Neil, Paul, and Joe was still fresh on my mind, and now that fate or fortune had delivered complete ownership back to me, I knew that giving up 51 percent of the operation would be giving up my ability to control my own destiny.

I had indeed been lucky, but I vowed to do everything possible to secure financing *and* retain control.

• • •

The universe stepped in again.

An associate suggested that I send a copy of the business plan to Gordon Jackson, a sheepskin tanner in Geelong, Australia. I called Gordon, and we had a long discussion about the business.

The Jackson family had a long history in the sheepskin-tanning business and was the world's largest supplier of catgut tennis strings under the Klipspringer brand. Their tannery in Geelong had a huge output, and Gordon was tied in with all of the skin sources.

I shared with Gordon my vision of UGG brand distribution in the States. He was enthused with my forecasted sales for the current season of three million dollars. We talked about manufacturers, styles, colors, soles, and other sourcing issues that go into the boot-manufacturing business. As we hung up, Gordon said he was very interested in investing in the business and was looking forward to reading the business plan.

I was on cloud nine! Finally, I had a prospective deal that made sense for everyone involved. Enthusiastically, I called George—and was met with a long silence. When he spoke, I didn't understand the ice in his voice. Recounting my conversation with Gordon, I told him we had the potential to finance the company, and George could get all the skins he needed for his production. On top of that, if we put the deal together, the Jacksons would help finance the entire operation and supply us both with credit until we could sell the boots in the United States.

George just said, "Well, I'll have to think about it."

Once again, I had that disquieting feeling—the opposite of goose bumps—that all was not well with Country Leather.

• • •

Paul walked into the office. "The L.L. Bean order has to ship by August fifteenth," he told me. Eight hundred and sixteen pairs of boots in a special brown color.

Since Country Leather was noncommittal, I sent a sample of the tall boot to Doug Price at Canterbury; he already had patterns from a previous order and a supply of UGG labels to stitch to the back of the boots as well as the ski-style rubber soles we needed.

Doug said he could produce the boots in a week and airfreight them to Anaheim . . . but how would we pay him? Because of the factoring deal imminent with MFC Financial, I didn't want to take ownership of the boots into our warehouse, so I said to Doug, "How about if I get L.L. Bean to make a new order directly to you, and you collect the payment from them?" He agreed. That week Doug arrived to see our situation firsthand and to look at the purchase orders. Steve Nitzberg sat in our meetings and convinced Doug that receivable financing was imminent with a company called MFC Financial, and the market was very real. We visited several of our best customers.

I think that enthusiasm for UGG was the tipping point for Doug. He made a leap of faith and guaranteed that he would instruct his factory to begin immediate production for nine thousand pairs, with a first delivery as soon as the first three thousand pairs were complete. In return, I promised him that his would be the first payment I made from any factoring arrangement we made. No documents were signed. Doug trusted me, I trusted him, and we both delivered on our promises.

Two weeks later, eight hundred and sixteen pairs of boots arrived on Friday. We worked through the weekend to ship them off to L.L. Bean. First shipping disaster of the season averted.

• • •

It had been eight days since I had sent the business plan, and I hadn't heard from Gordon Jackson, so I called him.

"I haven't received the business plan," he told me. "Don't make any decisions until I have time to look it over. In the meantime, I'm sending my US associate, Graeme Goodsir, to visit you and look over the business. He'll report to me what he thinks, then we'll take it from there."

Unbelievable. We had lost a valuable week. I couriered him another copy of the plan. The next day, Graeme called to arrange his visit, so I sent him a copy of the business plan and an estimated cash flow as well.

August was more than half over, and I knew our shipments to retailers were due to start at the beginning of September. I made another desperate call to George, to convince him that our imminent receivables financing was about to be signed with MFC Financial. He offered to send me $50,000 worth of product, to be partly prepaid from the export grant money, on the condition that I pay him immediately from the factoring receipts. I was happy with the deal, since at least this would fill in the sizes and styles we were low in until I could get fully financed.

• • •

Although we had not discussed defined roles for Paul and his wife, Maria, they had agreed to become employees and were indispensable to keeping the company afloat. We were desperate to move the remaining inventory out of Anaheim, but we had no money to pay Della. She finally agreed to accept a personal promissory note to be repaid, with interest, in six months. As Della and I signed the purchase documents, I was sure that Neil would have approved.

I rented a huge green truck. Paul, Maria, and I spent the day emptying the Anaheim warehouse. Despite the daunting financial hurdles ahead, the three of us shared optimism about a new chance to save UGG. We loaded the boxes of boots, trade-show materials, brochures, order forms, and everything we had accumulated building the business into the truck. Around 8 PM we finally hit the road, me in the truck, with Paul and Maria following in their fully laden car.

At one point, near Irvine, they overtook me and waved me over. It seems I had not tied the load down very well, and cardboard shipping cartons were blowing around as far back along the I-5 freeway as we could see, flipping in the air as cars passed.

By 11 PM the truck was off-loaded into our new home at Greg's warehouse, and we headed off to bed, me to my house, and Paul and Maria to the local Motel 6.

We'd spent the day in high spirits, like true entrepreneurs optimistic about our chance to start over again. The pieces were falling into place. Now that George Burcher and Doug Price had come through with our initial orders, we were going to meet our deliveries through mid-September. But what about October and November, our biggest shipping months?

I now had control of my own destiny. I'd not only bought out Della, but I had also signed notes with the Rhodes family to buy back their shares in UGG Imports, Inc. I was a sole owner once again.

Now, I just needed to sign up the factoring company and secure a deal with Gordon Jackson to shore up deliveries for the rest of the season

• • •

Dana was on the road writing orders daily, and our prebookings were around the two-million-dollar mark. She called in and told me that Thunderwear was telling everyone that UGG was out of business and that they were taking over the market.

"And get this, Brian," Dana said, "they're getting their boots from Country Leather."

I was steaming. Our showdown wasn't meant to go down this way! I always thought George and I would be having a conversation when his manufacturing capacity could not keep up with our sales, but to go behind my back? I was angry and couldn't wait for 8 AM in Albany so I could call him. It was a quick conversation.

"I've sold them only $20,000 worth of boots," he told me. "I have to protect myself, you know. If you send me cash from your CODs, I'll send you more product."

That was absurd. I needed the product to ship before I could collect COD revenue.

Graeme Goodsir, Gordon Jackson's envoy, arrived at our office. A tall, distinguished, upper-crust Australian, Graeme had formerly headed up the US operations for the Australian Beef Council and had a long-standing relationship with Gordon. Admitting that he had never heard of UGG, Graeme nonetheless knew business, and we spent a few days together investigating all the sales, administration, and inventory needs. His thirst for detail was exhausting, but eventually, he learned enough to recommend that the Jacksons get into the business with me and finance the operation.

A few days later, Gordon called with an offer to supply as many boots as we needed if we would send him letters of credit to secure the payments. *Oh no!* I thought. *Doesn't he get it?* Gordon was my last hope to get someone else to finance production. But now he was throwing it back on me to finance him.

For a day or two, I went into a mild depression. I hadn't had a good night's sleep for months. We had little cash, and I had been spending whatever cash came in to save face in the market, to show people that we were still alive and kicking, by running ads and booking trade shows. I was also paying a small salary to Paul and Maria.

Painfully aware of the obligation I had to provide for customers who I considered long-standing personal friends, I spent the weekend in contemplation, running over the ramifications of going out of business. By Sunday evening, I realized I was reacting to outside events as a victim of circumstance, so I boldly decided to take charge. My inner voice told me to embrace the uncertainties and challenge the illusion of defeat.

On Monday, I told Paul and Maria, "I'm going to Australia to see Gordon Jackson."

I pulled the orders for Mitch's Surf and Witt's Carlsbad Pipelines and loaded the car with their assortment of COD boots. South Coast Surf also took their shipment COD. I used the cash to buy a Qantas ticket to Melbourne.

Ignoring my seat assignment, I walked down the aisle scanning for a row of four empty seats. Near the back, I found them and prayed for the doors to close before someone came aboard with tickets for these seats. As soon as we began taxiing, I snapped the seat belt loosely around me and lay down. I have no memory of the plane taking off.

Fifteen hours later, I awoke with the bump of the wheels touching down in my homeland. I had missed breakfast. As we deplaned, I felt the most rested I had been in over three months.

I liked Gordon Jackson immediately. About five foot eight, he was round and balding with hard but humorous eyes. We quickly got down to negotiations. Gordon introduced me to his son, Bob, who ran the tennis string business, and then we met at the tannery with Graham, his son who ran that operation. I was fascinated by the tanning process and soon got used to the smell of the wet skins that had been salted to keep them from decaying in the elements.

On the first day, I saw them throw a batch of skins into a vat of dark brown dye; the skins came out with the leather dark brown and the fleece still white. The next day I saw them throw a batch of skins into another vat of dark brown dye; they came out with the dark brown fleece and white skins. I have never figured out the secrets of tanning.

The Jackson family was not in the boot manufacturing business, but they supplied skins to several companies that did make boots. The two sons ran the business, but Gordon, the father, had the final say. On his desk was a wooden plaque that read, *I reserve the right to change my mind.*

It quickly became clear Gordon just wanted to be a broker to source supply and send boots to the United States with guarantees of payment. I told him that was impossible, that I needed a partner to finance production and send shipments, with payment to be made after we collected from our customers. I had expected Gordon to take this position, despite his earlier interest during our phone calls to invest in our company.

I am a big believer in getting face-to-face with the people who are potential partners in my destiny. Spending personal time, especially meeting the various associates and even family of your potential partner and watching how they react with each other, can open doors into their character. They also get to learn about your personal life and assess your character, and more often than not, that observation can sway the course of a business deal.

There are many means of having face time with associates, like using video conferencing technology, but you can't take a computer out for lunch or home for dinner. The bottom line is that people still like to do deals with people.

Over the next three days, I saw Gordon waver back and forth, from absolute support to wanting to have nothing to do with export, and we never arrived at a solution. The best Gordon could offer was that he would finance the business if he had 51 percent of the deal, while I maintained that the UGG name was a valuable asset. He said that the trademark was of no value without his money, which was something I'd heard before from others. The truth is, in negotiations, he who has the cash has a decided advantage.

I asked him to keep in mind that it would mean $1.5 million in sales for his tannery, but he wasn't impressed with that either.

After the final swing of the Gordon pendulum, we agreed to form a company to include Graeme Goodsir (who had flown in for the meeting). Gordon said he would relax his demand for owning 51 percent of the company if I could prove that I had receivables financing. I was elated, because I was confident that Steve Nitzberg was on the brink of bringing MFC Financial on board, meaning a 50/50 deal with Gordon was doable.

As I departed, Graeme Goodsir asked what I was going to do in the meantime. I was out of options. I told him that Paul and I had already run the cash flow forecasts: we'd need $7,000 to stay alive for another month. Graeme, God bless him, opened his checkbook and wrote a check for $7,000 on the spot. As he handed it to me, he said, "I'll keep working with Gordon. It makes so much sense that I'm sure there's a way to make it happen."

In September 1988, we shipped to all of our major accounts from the product that had come in from Canterbury. The same month, we set up our booth at the action-sports trade show in Long Beach, where we had our first look at Thunderwear. I don't know who was most surprised: them, seeing UGG still alive and exhibiting, or me, seeing Thunderwear's full range of styles and colors matching the UGG line product by product, including the black and charcoal which George had told me were unavailable. It was finally clear that George had been playing me, which accounted for his lukewarm conversations with me and his indifference about my efforts to keep UGG alive.

By lunchtime on the first day, we had written an unprecedented $60,000 in orders. I'd kept an eye on the Thunderwear booth and was pleased to notice it was relatively quiet. I felt humbled by the loyalty of my regular customers. When I told them that Country Leather appeared to be doing an end run around me, they were all sympathetic. Pacific Sunwear came in with an order for $79,000. The total sales for the three days of the show were nearly $200,000.

Word must have gotten back to George that THUGGS wasn't putting UGG out of business after all. Shortly after the show, he called me and offered to supply me if I would give him equity in UGG. I passed on his offer, and he cut me off completely.

One of my traits has always been to trust people even, as some of my friends say, to a fault. Luckily, over the years, I have learned to fine-tune my intuition, so I don't go as far down the road with people that I am wary of before pulling back from negotiations. All year, since Neil's death, I had picked up on a bad vibe with George, but it was not until I saw the Thunderwear booth with all my designs and colors displayed that I had proof he had switched teams. Obviously, despite his offer to supply product for the rest of the season, there was no way I was going to be co-owners with someone who had not been up front with me. I was also glad that we had never signed any binding supply/distribution contracts to muddy the waters of our clean split.

Although the show orders seemed to be a huge victory, in fact, we had dug a deeper hole for ourselves. Now that George was out of the picture, we had only Canterbury to make product for us, and I knew their production was capped.

At that point, I knew we weren't going to make it through the season.

Back home, I broke the bad news to Laura, then called Gordon Jackson.

I told him we'd reluctantly decided to call it quits; George had cut our supply, and without boots to sell, it didn't make a difference how many orders we took. We had to shut the business down.

Gordon somberly wished us well, and we ended the call. He called back ten minutes later.

"Screw George Burcher," he told me. "I'll get you twenty thousand pairs. Send me the patterns and samples, and I'll make sure you get your product."

Just like that, we were back in business again.

I'm sure this call wouldn't have been made if I had not gone to meet Gordon face-to-face. Because I had been to his home, shared meals, and stayed with his son Graham, we had opportunities to get to know each other personally. In Australia, you don't stand by and watch someone beat up your mate without stepping in to help, even at the risk of being bloodied yourself. I'm sure that is why Gordon stepped in to help me in my scuffle with George.

Become friends with your customers and suppliers. Cooperation will beat out competition every time.

He didn't try to squabble about ownership or payment, and he didn't require anything in writing.

Gordon's main customer for boot-grade skins was Westhaven, a "sheltered workshop" manufacturing business in New South Wales that provided jobs for mentally and physically handicapped people. They had been making sheepskin boots for years, and there was little training necessary for them to switch to the UGG styles. We knew we would have to forgo the black and charcoal colors for the season, but we doubted that our customers would mind as long as they had UGG brand boots to sell. Gordon claimed they could make five thousand pairs a week.

• • •

The first storms of the West Coast's winter season began in October, and the phones began ringing with calls from customers saying, "We want our shipments early." Paul and I were elated. Kinney Shoes came in with a big order, and Conrad and I had to figure out how many boots we could really expect from Gordon to add to the regular shipments from Canterbury before we accepted more orders. Based upon his five-thousand-pair schedule, we decided to keep taking orders.

The factoring deal with MFC Financial that Steve Nitzberg had been working on finally came together, but only on two conditions: they insisted that we incorporate, and I would have to personally guarantee the advances. Because of this, UGG America, as part of Neil's estate, passed into history, and UGG International, Inc., came into existence. We immediately sent MFC a stack of our invoices—now their invoices—for the product we'd already shipped. Within a week, we received 80 percent of the invoices' value in cash from them. This buoyed up Gordon Jackson, and although he was still pushing for 51 percent of the company, we finally settled on a 50/50 deal, with Graeme Goodsir owning a percentage of the Jacksons' half.

As November rolled on, sending cash to Canterbury in New Zealand and Gordon Jackson in Australia felt really good. Both Doug and Gordon had gambled on me without any security whatsoever, and I had come through.

I'm not advocating going into deals without fully documenting the arrangements—I have always had a letter of intent as a minimum— but good business relationships are not made by the words on paper.

In a perfect world, the legal documents are filed away in a drawer, never to be used again because each party is living up to the original expectations. In our imperfect world, however, as a business grows and new staff comes on board who are not privy to the original intent, shortcuts are attempted, which requires pulling the documents back out and everyone reviewing the business's mission.

That being said, the most fulfilling deals are always those based on trust and completed with honesty.

Boot shipments were whirling through customs. As fast as they came in, we shipped them through to customers. Now that we had cash flow, Conrad Mouton came on full-time, and I was finally able to relax, knowing that we had competent billing and accounting procedures. Paul and Maria Bussmann kept on top of the sales and commissions.

• • •

At last, nine months after Neil's life insurance claim had been made, Maynard Kartvedt called. "We have to be in L.A. next Wednesday," he said. "We finally have a meeting with Transamerica Life." Maynard had threatened to sue them, so now there would be a settlement conference.

After a contentious session the following week, their attorneys offered $200,000 to settle. We accepted. My thoughts went back to the day we wrote the life insurance policy and I thought to myself again, *Neil must have known.* I paid Maynard his commission and then cut a check to pay off the note to Della.

Bless Neil, who had provided for us both.

George Burcher had one thousand pairs of boots with UGG labels stitched on them, so he called to see if we would take them, but only for cash. Paul offered to guarantee a letter of credit and put $45,000 in the bank to secure it. When the boots arrived in the United States, our customs broker mixed up the paperwork and shipped our one thousand pairs of UGG brand boots to THUGGS, at the same time shipping two thousand pairs of THUGGS to us. I called Thunderwear and offered to bring their boots to their warehouse in San Clemente.

When I arrived, I was staggered to see boots everywhere—every style and color including the black and charcoal George had denied us. As I drove home, at first I was furious that George had sworn to me that he couldn't get the colored skins. Then I began to wonder why the THUGGS warehouse still had so much product stacked up when we couldn't keep boots for a day. A warm, contented feeling began to come over me, and I thanked God for the loyalty of my customers.

On New Year's Eve, Laura and I celebrated the survival of the company. Against seemingly insurmountable odds, we had survived the onslaught of a hostile competitor, moved the business to a new warehouse only minutes from home, brought on a new friend and supplier in Gordon Jackson, received an unlikely payout from an insurance company that enabled me to pay off Della, obtained receivables financing to accelerate our cash flow, and to top it off, I owned 100 percent of the new company, UGG International, Inc., which gave me flexibility to bring in Gordon as a full partner in the new year. But this was only a small part of our conversation. Mostly we talked about our family, which consisted of me, Laura, Erika, and the baby Laura was carrying.

Westhaven Industries press release.

CHAPTER 10

GROWING PAINS

"Get out in front. And run faster."
1989—Sales $2 million

The mid-teen years confront a young person with the hardest lessons and steepest challenges of life yet, but if everything that has come before has created a solid foundation, these obstacles are not insurmountable.

Paul Bussmann, Conrad Mouton, and I looked with amazement down the canyon we had somehow scaled in 1988. Then we turned to face the new plateau that stretched before us. As New Year's Day 1989 arrived, UGG was in poor shape, yet we were alive, in good spirits, and ready to rebuild.

I recalled thinking over the ten previous years that when we finally hit a million dollars in sales, there would be so much cash flowing in that things would be easy. I was beginning to figure out why this was not so.

With this in mind, our first order of business was to shore up immediate financing for supply and begin the process of assuring consistent deliveries for next season. I headed to Australia to meet with Gordon Jackson. On the way, I stopped over in Sydney to meet with Peter Raffin, the new owner of UGHS.

In a year-round business, it is normal to *turn around* inventory (where you buy a certain amount of inventory and sell it all) four or even six times a year. This way, you get to use the profits from each "turn" to purchase the next round of inventory, and use the balance to pay for overhead expenses, such as salaries, office costs, etc. But we only had one turn of inventory in a very short three-month window. Although these three months were very profitable, it was never enough to pay for a year's expenses. An added problem was that we were beginning to double our sales every year, which meant we *had* to source outside capital to keep up with the extra inventory purchase. The rule of industry seems to be that even a year-round business cannot grow from internal cash flow if it exceeds a 20 percent growth each year.

Peter was large in all ways: large physical presence, a booming voice, and big visions for sheepskin boots in America. He wasn't happy with sales the previous season. He still wanted to sell the UGHS business to me, but I told him we were first going to get our own supply line in place before we could look at what Peter was offering.

Flying down to meet Gordon Jackson in Melbourne, I dreamed of all the good things we could do if we had solid capital. When Gordon and I made a quick trip to the tannery in Geelong, I pulled out several pairs of the boots Westhaven had shipped to us before Christmas. The boots were of moderate quality, typical of all the product we received from them. We had accepted them without complaint during the frenzy of December deliveries, but now I made it clear that poor quality does not survive long in the

US retail market. I brushed aside a few "She'll be right, mate" comments and insisted we meet at the Westhaven factory in Dubbo the next week.

After a quick weekend with my parents in Canberra, I met Gordon and his son Graham in Dubbo, a small city known as the Crossroads of New South Wales. As we toured the Westhaven factory there, I pulled out my samples from the previous year and pointed out all the blemishes in the skins.

"That's Graham's problem," the Westhaven production manager said. "He ships us the skins." I saw Graham wince, but he couldn't refute the truth in that comment.

We moved on to the patterns that had been poorly copied from Canterbury, with sloppy gluing. We had to instruct them not to fold the tall boots prior to shipping, because they arrived with creases halfway up the boot that we couldn't fix in the United States. Ironically, a few boxes of boots that we had returned to Westhaven had arrived a few days earlier, so we had them brought into the conference room. More than five-dozen pairs had been rejected because the stitching up the sides was not tied off—if you pulled on the thread, you could unravel the entire side of the boot. Gordon was furious, claiming that it was our problem and we should fix them, but I held my ground. After a day of wrangling, we agreed on a quality-control checklist covering both skin quality and production specs. Gordon and I flew back to Melbourne that evening.

Gordon and I now had to settle on the financial terms of our new relationship, considering it had already been in effect for a few months with no paperwork whatsoever. The 50/50 deal was still intact, and now it was time to draft the formal documentation for UGG International, Inc. Try as I might, I could not get Gordon to commit to a consistent cash infusion that would cover a systematic production of boots. He wanted his 50 percent of the stock of UGG International, Inc., without any guarantee to pay for product. I didn't want to leave Melbourne without a completed agreement, but we were at a stalemate. Without signing over the shares, I felt as though I was leaving town with a "She'll be right mate; we'll send the product when you need it."

We both knew we had a huge opportunity, so we would just have to make the details work.

On my way home, I called in on Canterbury Sheepskin in New Zealand, where Doug Price was ready to go forward. He knew that manufacturing had to be continuous to be profitable, and he knew precisely what capacity and speed was available to us. He agreed to commit to twenty thousand pairs on the condition that I could guarantee letters of credit each month beginning in July. *Okay*, I thought, *I have five months to get Gordon to commit to funding the company.*

•   •   •

Back home in California, at the warehouse, things were clicking along nicely. Conrad and Paul were working well together to cover the sales and financial administration, so I left immediately to visit some big hitters on the East Coast. L.L. Bean committed to buy again, and I picked up an order for eighteen hundred pairs from Thom McAn. Their buying office in Worcester, Massachusetts, had an entrance lobby at least a hundred yards long. All along one wall was a museum of shoes, some from China and Egypt dating back two thousand years.

In New York, I entered the gilded lobby of the classic Woolworth building on my way up to visit the Kinney buyer, Jay O'Brien. He told me they'd had good sell-through in California, but the main buyers hadn't jumped yet. He described to me a whole contingent of brokers within the shoe industry who were always on the lookout for a hot new category of products supplied by a variety of vendors, so product can be sourced at deep discounts in return for big volumes.

"Because of you, shearling is being sourced all over the world right now," he said. "Don't even attempt to match the others on price. My advice is to keep to the high end of the market, and keep the quality and brand name intact for the next two seasons."

It took a week or so for this to sink in. I still felt that UGG was insignificant in the shoe industry, and our marketing efforts were so localized to the surf and ski enthusiasts that we wouldn't be on the national footwear radar. But Jay was right. Next season, the shoe shelves were full of sheepskin product from slippers to clogs. All were cheap and had no staying power. It widened my horizons, knowing that our efforts had established a valid category, and spurred me on to keep doing exactly what we were doing.

• • •

In March at the Ski Show, orders topped $400,000.

Conrad ran some cash flow forecasts; all of them showed a long, lean summer ahead. We laid off our warehouse shipper. Dana Hatch also resigned, so I went back on the road.

After visiting Santa Cruz, Portola, and Carmel, I headed inland toward the mountains to visit Track and Trail, a mall chain. They were headquartered in a massive warehouse filled with outdoor gear. As I left the building with an order for forty-five hundred pairs, I began to understand at last the power of the outdoor market and now knew why my friends Jeff and Steve from *Action Sports Retailer* magazine had been promoting their *Outdoor Retailer* magazine and *Outdoor* trade shows.

In May, a résumé came across my desk from Tom McGraw, who seemed to be my clone. I had been spending so much time on the details of doing all the sales, accounting, and warehouse operations that I wasn't spending enough time on planning and growing. Despite the fact that our cash flow was minimal, I hired Tom as a sales manager. A tall, athletic, smart, and personable entrepreneur with a passion for surfing, Tom was already a fan of the UGG product. He immediately took on the job of organizing our action-sports accounts, relieving me of many of my road-sales obligations. More important, he also took over organization of the trade shows. His first task was to transfer our inventory to another new warehouse, this time in Carlsbad.

In early June, Laura gave birth to our second daughter, Kelley. Erika took to her little sister immediately. Laura and I owned our house in Encinitas, so we spent the slow months of summer planning to add an extra room for the girls.

• • •

As I began to intensify my efforts to get the supply stream flowing, I continued to meet resistance from Gordon's changing moods. Sales were coming in, Conrad Mouton had the administrative controls developing, and Paul had his ski-market sales force clicking. Nonetheless, Gordon was vacillating between sending us 50,000 pairs and cutting us off completely, even threatening that he wanted out of the whole affair.

After my frantic calls, Gordon sent thirteen cartons of boots in August. Luckily for us, his son Bob was on a sales visit to the United States, and he happened to stop at our warehouse just as the cartons arrived from Westhaven. Bob took note of the fact we were forced to ration boots to our customers, and heard the phones ringing endlessly with calls from customers pleading for boots. He called his father the same day to affirm that what I had been telling Gordon was true: we were being crippled from lack of supply.

Westhaven was given the directive to ship everything they had on hand and to go into maximum production. Finally we were back on track—but we were two months behind, and I knew we would not catch up. Conrad and I matched our current sales orders against our expected deliveries. We would be throwing away sales of about thirty thousand pairs we could not provide. Tom sent a letter to all of our customers to cut off new orders on October 31. By the end of August, nine thousand pairs arrived . . . and were gone within a week.

For the first time, the Outdoor Retailer show produced good sales. This new industry that Steve and Jeff had been trying to get off the ground for four years was in its toddler stage. We hired a photographer to produce some images of our boots being worn in true-to-life settings, "inviting readers into the scene." He captured a spectacular shot of a young family with dad pulling his daughter on a sled through a pristine Colorado outdoor scene. It was an instant hit. The new wholesome family image finally replaced the UGG Girl image that had soured female buyers for so many years. We would reap the benefits of their grudging acceptance of us at the next Ski Show.

In September 1988, I saw my first snowboarding magazine. I bought a board of my own and was hooked on the sport within a week. I'd grown up surfing and reading surf magazines, and just looking at their photos, I could feel the g-forces in each bottom turn or cutback that surfers make in big waves. The moment I saw the cover of *Transworld Snowboarding*, I felt the same rush.

"Snowboarding is going to be the next big thing," I told the crew. Although snowboards were allowed in only three ski areas in the United States at the time, I imagined a day when every resort would see snowboarding's potential to revive a flagging ski industry, and we began to strategize how we might get into the snowboarding market with the UGG brand.

We had watched footwear companies like Nike and Reebok expand their markets by adding apparel to their core lines, offering add-on sales opportunities to their loyal customers. Since our boots were already being sold by ski shops to potential boarders, it seemed a logical step for us to offer technical snowboard apparel to the early adopters in this new market.

Paul had great contacts within the industry, so he called Mireille, a skiwear designer he knew who had also watched the embryonic sport grow in Europe and was looking at ways of taking advantage of this new market. We sent her designs to Paul's contact at Evergreen Sewing, to get samples in time for the next ski show, and a graphic designer came up with a young, fresh logo that was a radical departure from our old-timer boot image—and perfect for a young and radical new sport.

• • •

The volume of boots Westhaven had promised was not coming through, so I planned a trip to Australia to see firsthand what the problem was. When I called Gordon Jackson, he forbade me to talk to any manufacturers.

One thing I've learned over my thirty-plus years in business: When someone insists that you not talk with another party involved in a business deal, look out! There's almost always some kind of hidden agenda.

I decided Gordon's directive made it all the more important that I go to Australia to get a realistic expectation of our capacity for filling orders the rest of the season. We were already eight weeks behind, so I had to know when to cut off our sales.

At first Gordon was apologetic for the undersupply, but as soon as I brought up quality, he flipped and challenged me to buy him out. His volatility astonished me. Later I spoke with his son Graham, who admitted they did not have the ability to exceed twenty-two hundred pairs per week; this was not what his father had told me. I told Graham I was going to visit other manufacturers in Sydney and asked if he would be able to supply skins to them.

"Not while my family owns the tannery," he said.

I became determined that next season I would raise enough independent capital to buy Gordon out, but our conversation had begun the wheels turning in Graham's brain too, and he would soon become just as determined to find a way to buy the tannery from his family. Graham saw the big picture. He was aware that Australia was a tiny market compared with the United States. He knew that for manufacturing to be profitable, it needed to be consistent and predictable. The driving factor in being predictable was that proper financing had to be in place in order to get the best prices for skins to begin the flow, right through to steady manufacturing, where employees could be trained for each stage: cutting, stitching, gluing, and packing and shipping. Our previous on again/off again cycle had to be broken.

From Sydney, I called Conrad Mouton in California for an update on sales.

"Forty-five thousand pairs," he told me.

"That's exactly how many pairs I think we can get by Christmas from here, so tell Tom to cut off orders."

Our reorders for November and December each year had traditionally been 50 percent of our preseason total, so we would be forfeiting sales of about twenty thousand pairs for the season. Our short supply was a disaster in the making, not just due to lost sales from reorders, but also because it would spur other brands to come into the market as competitors.

In retrospect, we came to view the new competitors as a blessing. Until that point, UGG was a unique, much-sought-after brand. With the advent of several competitors—including UGHS, THUGGS, Scaffa, Qwaruba, and others—we had inadvertently created a new product category. I began to see the wisdom of what the Kinney Shoes buyer had told me six months earlier. The arrival of a new category brought strong new credibility for risk-averse buyers for the biggest chains. Basically, small niche products will only be stocked by the smaller specialty stores, but once a product catches on and competitors proliferate, it becomes safer for the larger buyers to get on board. A rising tide lifts all boats, so they say.

Our mission intensified: stay out in front of our competitors and keep running faster!

By the time I got back to San Diego, Graham Jackson had worked some magic and somehow convinced his father that the best thing for the family's factory was for them to finance the entire production of boots from several manufacturers, while Graham supplied them all with the skins from his own tannery. At last, UGG had secure financing.

•   •   •

November and December became "all hands on deck" months for the warehouse. Our new shipping manager, Jack, handled the chaos of receiving, unpacking, sorting, filling the shelves, pulling the orders, and preparing shipments to customers, while Conrad and I spent long evenings catching up on the paperwork and accounting.

Conrad handed me the October financials showing a profit—that glorious word—of $140,000, the first meaningful profit we had made since Doug Jensen and I started the business ten years before, in 1979. I relayed the good news to Gordon and Graham, knowing November and December would be even more profitable. As soon as we collected the receivables, we'd be able to pay off all their financing and hopefully go into next season with a new attitude.

As great as this victory was, it had a bittersweet element to it. Both Conrad and I knew that if production had started earlier, we might have made another $300,000 profit, and I still wasn't sure that Gordon was going to step up to the plate with earlier financing next season. We both agreed that we had to raise sufficient and certain financing for next season.

With this in mind, I sent the final year-end accounts to Alan Greenway with a note: "We have to talk soon."

Center: Cool family-friendly winter image. *Bottom left*: Snowboard logo.

CHAPTER 11

HIGH SCHOOL

Capital, cash flow, and the Christmas nightmare
1990—Sales $2.2 million

*The late-teen years find solid relationships forming that may or may not last for-
ever—or even through college. Peer pressure begins to fade, a more worldly view
of things appears, and life goals are sought.*

Due to both lack of deliveries from manufacturers and our poor financing, we had walked away from orders for about thirty thousand
pairs of boots—$1.5 million sales—in each of the two previous years. We
vowed that in 1990 our focus would be on securing the capital to preorder
inventory.

• • •

Tom McGraw called a few of his ski-market buyer contacts, and we met
with them in an informal focus group. We all agreed that the ski industry

had lost much of the excitement it once had. The young counterculture ski enthusiasts from the 70s and 80s were fast approaching middle age and had kids in school and tight budgets. Business at ski resorts had been declining steadily for a few years. The booming "teenage" years for the ski industry were behind it. Skiing was now a sport for older folks, at least in the minds of the next generation of consumers.

I sensed the vibrancy of the young snowboarding phenomenon, even though there was tremendous resistance from skiers and ski areas. Only three areas allowed snowboarders on the lifts: Big Bear in California, a small hill in Park City, Utah, and one in Vermont. Snowboarding was just beginning the toddler stage of its growth, and we all agreed that we should ride the wave of expansion. To get maximum attention for the UGG brand in this market, we needed to be front-runners. Since there was no dominant clothing line catering to snowboarders, if we launched into the market with an UGG apparel line, the boot brand would gain credibility by osmosis. The more beers we drank, the more creative our ideas and our new vision became.

Following Steve's advice from back in 1979 that "It's not how big you are, but how big you are perceived to be," we envisioned a launch that would make a huge splash, including a trade show booth resembling a snow cave.

Leaving Tom to put together the snow cave from big, white polystyrene blocks, Conrad, Paul, and I got into the accounting. As our normal collections for the ski and surf accounts came in, we would be able to pay the final bills to our manufacturers and to our factor.

And then in the middle of January, the dreaded Santa Ana winds came in from the desert and warm temperatures hit all over the country. Our cash flow slowed to a stop. UGG would be at the tail end of every checkbook in the retail stores, so we scrambled to call our customers, offering deep discounts in return for COD deliveries, but the surf shop mentality had already switched to summer.

We defaulted on our remaining $90,000 payment to Gordon Jackson in Australia, and despite the fact that we had sent him nearly a million dollars over the previous three months, he wasn't happy. I had discontinued my own commissions when I became an owner again, and without them, money was tight in my household.

We were owed more than $200,000 by our retailers, and although we had a profitable season, our lack of timely capital exposed our vulnerability. Conrad and I put the finishing touches on yet another, updated business plan and I hit the road to find potential investors. Every bank that I approached was indifferent to the profit we had made on paper and offered the familiar refrain, "UGG is a fad. Yes, you had a good year, but UGG won't be around much longer." I approached several venture capital groups without success, and I also gave the updated business plan to Alan Greenway, which he sent off to his business partner in Australia.

• • •

We had seven months before the next shipping cycle to our retailers, and not wishing to waste a moment, I flew to Melbourne and went down to the tannery in Geelong to meet with Graham Jackson. He confided that he knew the lost sales hadn't been our fault, and that he was getting tired of his father's promises and reversals that threw any plans for streamlining production into chaos. He'd been researching how to buy the tannery from his family. We agreed that I should talk to Gordon about financing the overall production of boots but leave it up to Graham to put together a stable of manufacturers. Graham would act as agent/buyer for UGG International, sourcing production from reliable manufacturers to which he would ship skins for production.

• • •

While I was away, Tom had done the action sports and the outdoor shows and once again, prebookings were strong. Short shipping in the previous season was definitely an incentive for stores to order early, yet this was small consolation for missing so many sales in the previous season.

We made a huge impression at the Ski Show in Las Vegas at the end of March. Our new twenty-by-twenty booth was our largest and most spectacular yet, and UGG was one of the busiest booths at the show. Because of the warm winter and early spring, many retailers had cut back on buying the traditional brands and were looking for something new. Mireille and Nick from Evergreen Sewing had produced a fabulous line of snowboard wear.

The obvious snowboard image of our booth was a big departure from all of the traditional skiwear companies, who looked the same as they had during the previous season. We had six tables in our booth, and I was amazed at how many times all six were in use by our reps and their customers. I learned later through Paul, who was a member of the Ski Industries Association, that about six apparel brands decided to go out of business after that show due to lack of orders, while we had written close to a half-million dollars in snowboard gear our first time out of the gate. As we hoped, the flow of customers greatly increased our boot sales as well.

Looking at the company from the sales and marketing side, things could not have been better. From the financial side, it could not be worse. The cash flow forecast confirmed we were in deep trouble. I knew I'd have to go on the road to chase down delinquent accounts. I asked Tom and Paul to call around to see if we could close out the forty-five hundred pairs of boots that had been stuck in transit over Christmas and were still in our warehouse after three months.

Because the $200,000 that should have been in our bank account was still unpaid by our customers, we found ourselves in another cash crunch.

At the end of the month, I was facing one of the low points in my whole UGG career. I had to evaluate the necessity of each employee. I tried to do it sensitively, but the process ultimately backfired on me.

Since he was crucial to keeping the reps and sales effort going, Tom was indispensable. He had two small daughters, and because I was in the same situation, I knew he couldn't stay on for less than he was already earning. Although Paul and Maria were also valuable and had helped me through the UGG America transition, I thought they might be able to get by with fewer hours. Jack had told me he could get a different warehouse job and offered to come in at night on an hourly basis as needed. Conrad offered to come in just two days a week for a monthly consulting fee of $2,000.

The remaining office and warehouse staff had to be let go. I asked Conrad to cut checks to reflect this. Then, telling only Conrad, I went to the bank and borrowed $12,000 on my personal credit card and deposited it to cover the week's payroll.

I had planned to gather the staff at the end of the day, to hand out checks and regretfully outline the changes, but just before the end of business on this cold and rainy evening, Conrad gave out the checks before I called the meeting. Before I knew what was going on, everyone had compared their checks and knew something unpleasant had happened. They stormed my office demanding to know what was going on. Paul and Maria resigned on the spot, and everyone else was railing against me for not having the guts to come and lay them off personally. Almost at once, the office was empty, and I sat listening to the rain pelting on the windows. I couldn't help feeling that I had inadvertently betrayed Paul and Maria Bussmann, the two most dedicated UGG employees who had saved the company only two years previously.

I didn't blame Conrad for jumping the gun. I should have made a priority of talking to the staff as a group, outlining the reasons for the cutbacks. Instead, I was on the phone, putting out other fires with creditors, which seemed more urgent at the time. I've since learned the difference between urgent *and* important. *Since I was going to impact the lives of several employees, it was far more important that I deal with them first, because the creditors would have still been there the next day. I have tried to make compassion for my employees a priority since then.*

It was now mid-July and the manufacturers were pressing Graham Jackson to tell them how many boots to make. Graham had bought the tannery business from his family but, in doing so, had cut himself off from their backing to finance production. He was relying on me to get new investors. Although we had given production orders to Graham as soon as we made sales, he had been unwilling to authorize the manufacturers to begin until he was sure we could supply letters of credit from our pending financing sources. Unfortunately, our pending financing was, so far, nonexistent. With his factory at a standstill, I convinced him to fly to the United States to go over our situation.

First, I took him around to visit our best customers, where he saw that our sales orders represented a very real and urgent demand. Convinced, he directed Westhaven to release two thousand pairs that had been produced after Christmas. Combined with the forty-five hundred pairs we had in our warehouse, we had just enough boots to be able to ship orders due on September 1.

Next, since I felt sure that Alan Greenway was close to making a decision to come into the business, I set up a meeting to introduce Graham and Alan. The two hit it off. Alan agreed to renew his efforts with his partner in Sydney to move forward with a financing package, and to show good faith, Graham agreed to call in twenty thousand skins from his brokers on credit, and to begin sending orders to our manufacturers. I agreed to prepare a term sheet describing a new investment for Alan, and to begin negotiations to buy Gordon Jackson's interest back.

A *term sheet* is a document that sets out the various terms of a pending transaction. It usually covers what the investor will get for his money, including what percentage of the company, the timing, and the obligations of both parties to put a deal together. Similar to a letter of intent, it becomes a document that the lawyers can use as a draft to prepare full documentation of the deal. A *promissory note* (also just called a *note*) is a promise to pay a certain amount to someone, with the timing, due dates, interest rates, and any guarantees made by the issuer in return for some value (in my case, the purchase of Gordon's stock).

The next few weeks were a blur. Faxes were flying back and forth to Alan's partner, Ken Bailey, in Sydney, and daily phone calls with Gordon Jackson. He wanted to be paid in cash, but I steadfastly refused, offering instead a note with a personal guarantee to pay him from my share of profits in the upcoming season.

On the last day of July, Conrad tallied up the sales orders, which totaled $3.3 million (about sixty thousand pairs).

Nonetheless, by August, my credit cards were maxed out, and I could no longer pay wages that way. Laura and I agreed to take out a loan against our house, and I banked the entire proceeds, $33,390, into the UGG bank account.

I was exhausted. It was becoming more and more difficult to keep up the appearance of having things under control, when in reality I had no idea how to get enough boots for the season.

I shopped our business plan around to everyone I could think of. In keeping with the logic that our ideal investor would come from within the action-sports industry, I sent a letter to Doug Otto, the founder and president of Deckers Outdoor Corporation. Doug had started out in the footwear business with his triple-decker neoprene flip-flops back in 1979. He had licensed several surfing brands, including Lightning Bolt, which was a big brand in the surfing community. He had just licensed a nylon and rubber sandal called TEVA that was targeted to the hiking, climbing, and river-rafting segment of the outdoor industry. Doug showed some interest, but said he was too busy with his new acquisition to spend time reading it.

During this time, Tom and I also sat down for our own little two-man think-tank and began adding up our assets. We had over sixty-five thousand pairs of boots on order, and could count on another twenty thousand pairs of reorders assuming we had the product by Christmas. Our brand loyalty was tremendous. The national sales force was clicking—in California, we owned 75 percent of the market—and our trade show and advertising presence over the past ten years reflected the increasing power of the UGG brand. We had begun shipping the regular COD accounts, so we knew we could survive through September and October.

On the downside, we had to get product or nothing else mattered.

Our financing leads seemed to be moving at the speed of molasses. August rolled into September, and I'd heard nothing from potential investors for a week. I was exhausted from the stress of dealing with the clashing personalities and from keeping all of our retailers believing that everything was under control. Tom and I were on the brink of writing a letter to our customers advising them that we were closing sales for the season, UGG was sold out, when the phone rang.

Alan asked, "Can you meet me? I want to introduce you to Chuck Kaiser."

Chuck was a CPA who had recently retired from a large international accounting firm and Alan had asked him to look over the UGG business plan.

Around six feet tall, immaculately dressed in a suit and tie, with olive skin and dark hair, Chuck told me he had studied our business plan and had to admit that UGG showed a lot of promise. Alan took over, explaining that he and Chuck would like to create a new company to be called UGG Holding, Inc., and put up money to bankroll letters of credit so production could get started, on the condition that Chuck be allowed to look over my shoulder as the business progressed.

Thinking to myself that this was Alan's way of making sure someone was watching his money, I jumped at the chance. My intuition told me to be wary of Chuck, but UGG came first. We had three hundred retailers to keep happy. I had held out as long as possible, but to make this deal happen, I reluctantly agreed to take less than 51 percent of the new company's stock.

I personally arranged to pay out Gordon Jackson and Graeme Goodsir.

Graham Jackson was relieved to hear the news and immediately sent production orders to our team of manufacturers. Next, I asked Conrad Mouton to come back on full-time and brought on a new warehouse manager. Last, I called Doug Price at Canterbury Sheepskin, who committed to go into full production while the financing was in the works.

To get Chuck and Alan more engaged with UGG, I took them along to ASR as observers, certain they'd be impressed by the strong presence and loyal following UGG had in this market—but this was not to be! Neither Alan (in his late fifties and very conservative) nor Chuck (a New York–born accountant) could see past the orange, yellow, green, and blue hair of action-sport enthusiasts, or the nose piercings and earrings sported by the young skateboard and snowboard pros who hung out in the booths of their sponsors.

Alan and Chuck both left within the first hour, telling me on their way out, "This isn't the right environment for UGG." Despite the fact that 95 percent of all the exhibitors and attendees were perfectly normal looking, my new partners were in shock, as if they'd just discovered they were bank-rolling a street gang. I remember thinking, *This isn't going to be easy. They have no idea what it has taken to build the loyal following we have.*

Despite the end-of-show total showing we'd set a new company record in orders, I felt uneasy about the direction our marketing was likely to take if Alan and Chuck had their way. My fears were confirmed the next day when Chuck announced that he and Alan had made the decision to eliminate the snowboard line as soon as possible. Alan summed up what the trade show had taught them: "Those kids are punks, and snowboarding will never catch on."

For the first twelve years, I had seemed to be battling outside forces in order to grow the business.. I was soon to find that most of my battles would now be fought within the company. In my mind, I knew the business, and I naïvely thought that the investors would follow my lead in operational matters. Being a sophisticated investor, Alan formed a board of directors with Alan, Chuck, and I as members. However, Chuck was Alan's appointee, so I soon learned that what Alan wanted was always the outcome of any vote. In the vast majority of matters, Alan's position was solid, but his appointment of several friends, especially in the marketing department, who did not understand our customers and product, made things difficult for the team. I had held out for years on giving up 51 percent of the business so that I could ultimately call the shots when it came to day-to-day operational matters. And now, being a minority on the voting board in day-to day matters was just as debilitating.

Very few start-ups begin with a formal board of directors, partly because of the cost, but more commonly because the entrepreneur is making judgment calls and snap decisions inherent in the early phases. When the founders realize that they need to look at things from a broader perspective, they will look to friends and associates running more established business to act as a board of advisors. It is generally when a business gets so large that it needs the expert advice without the taint of any conflict of interest, that they budget for, and retain an outside board of directors of various numbers to suit the needs of investors, banks, and the like.

Three weeks went by and there were still no letters of credit set up for Graham. I learned from Alan that Chuck was unable to fund his capital contribution.

"This is unacceptable," I told Alan. "Every day without financing is losing us hundreds of pairs of boots. This is going to leave us in exactly the same mess as last season."

• • •

September drifted into October, and because Chuck could not come up with his share of the capital, the letters of credit were still stalled. Chuck and his lawyer were still fighting with his former employer over his payout, and Alan wasn't going to move forward with his share of the funding until Chuck contributed his capital. We had incorporated the new company, UGG Holdings, Inc., and I had already agreed on the terms to buy out Gordon's and Graeme Goodsir's portions of UGG International. I woke every morning with a sense of dread, knowing we were facing a repeat of the previous season's failure to have inventory when it came to Christmas shipping. Graham Jackson called to say the factories had been idle for two weeks since they'd finished the combined twenty thousand pairs he had ordered based on good faith and Chuck's promises. Doug Price also called to say he had shut down his factory for the same reason. With ten thousand pairs ready to ship, he asked, "Where are the letters of credit?"

Tom and I decided to send a memo to our retail accounts cutting off new orders until further notice. Then we called an urgent meeting with Alan in which I conveyed the desperation felt by our manufacturers and, for that matter, our own UGG team.

Alan finally took action. He loaned Chuck his initial investment of $100,000, opened a new bank account with $200,000, and guaranteed a line of credit with the bank to generate letters of credit. I convinced him that this would be all we needed, since, once the product shipped, we could bankroll additional production from our cash flow.

It was now the first week of November in 1990. The good news was that the factories began sending us everything they had completed, and they resumed production. The bad news was that we had missed out on five weeks of production, and Conrad calculated that we would not be able to satisfy all the orders we had on hand before Christmas.

We received thirty thousand pairs into the warehouse, requiring new employees to unpack, label, sort, and ship.

In the midst of this pandemonium, Gary, the owner of Thunderwear, called with more disturbing news. He told me that George Burcher was sending boots into the United States under the brand Country Leather UGG Boots and had cut Gary off. Gary suggested we team up to stop him.

After I'd given him a firm no and hung up, I was in disbelief that he would turn to me as an ally. I smiled at the poetic justice of the situation. As for Country Leather, we'd face off with George on our own terms, once things slowed down.

And then, at the worst possible moment, we got another phone call.

Four weeks prior to Christmas, John, a junior buyer for Nordstrom in the Houghton Plaza Mall in downtown San Diego, called me to place an order for a dozen pairs of boots, explaining that he had a discretionary-buy budget for products that might sell well locally. He picked up his order from our warehouse on Friday afternoon. By noon on Saturday, he was calling to order two-dozen pairs each for the Houghton Plaza, Fashion Valley, and Escondido stores—seventy-two pairs. We didn't have that many pairs in stock, so I told him he could have them the following week from the five thousand pairs arriving from Westhaven.

Three weeks before Christmas, John picked up the seventy-two pairs on Friday. Saturday afternoon, he called wanting to pick up four-dozen more pairs for each of the three stores—144 pairs! Again I told him he'd have to wait until the following week.

Two weeks before Christmas, John picked up the 144 pairs on Friday afternoon, but by this time I was feeling guilty about short-shipping our best surf-shop customers. When John called at noon the next day asking for four hundred more pairs for each store, I had to tell him, "Sorry. No more boots this season. See you at the trade show next March."

Three days before Christmas. What a nightmare!

Westhaven had shipped only twenty-two hundred pairs in each of the previous three weeks when we'd wanted five thousand pairs a week.

I went into the warehouse to supervise the shipping. I grabbed the paperwork and started with our most loyal accounts.

I ran through E.T. Surf's order:

Short Natural, size 7: 17 pairs—I marked it for what we could send: 7.

Short Natural, size 8: 22 pairs—we could only manage 8.

Short Natural, size 9: 19—I knocked it down to 6.

I hated it. I grit my teeth at having to short one of my longtime customers as I continued through his order, every style and size the same thing.

Witts Surf: Same thing

Jack's Surf: Same thing.

More than half of the twenty-two hundred pairs we had on hand went to our top six stores. The remaining hundred or so accounts got an average of ten pairs each.

The day before Christmas, local surf shop owners showed up at the warehouse to scavenge any boots they could find, but the warehouse floor was empty.

Exhausted, we shut down the warehouse for the holiday. Before I left, I cleared my answering machine. The final message was from Eddie Talbot, the "E.T." of E.T. Surf, our very first customer when Doug and I had started the business eleven years ago.

"Brian, I'll continue to do business with you," Eddie said in the message, "but I never want to talk to you again." All I could do was shrug. I felt empty and exhausted.

Laura and I had arranged to have a pre-Christmas dinner with her parents at a restaurant in Carlsbad called Niemans. Right across the street was Witt's Carlsbad Pipelines. I knew I should stop in to apologize for the short shipment, but also there was a good chance I'd get punched out by Witt. I picked up Erika, my three-and-a-half-year-old, excused myself, and walked across the street holding her as my shield. When I walked in, Witt took one look at me and said curtly, "Come outside."

Shit, I thought. *He's going to punch me anyway.*

"Do you realize how many crying mothers I've had in my store today?" he raged. "You promised me you'd catch up on the shipments, so I kept taking orders. Now I've turned away a hundred moms whose major gift to their kids was supposed to be sheepskin boots!"

I learned a valuable lesson that evening. My blind optimism had kept the UGG dream alive throughout a year of incredible hardship, but my blind optimism had also worked against me. Westhaven had promised to get five thousand pairs to us weekly, but every shipment had been twenty-two hundred pairs and a promise: "Next week you'll have the full shipment." Now we had short-shipped every customer in an attempt to spread the boots as widely as possible and keep everyone happy, only to alienate many of them.

In retrospect, we should have cut off new orders back in November, but my optimism had outweighed my common sense.

It was a very hard decision to ship to Nordstrom, knowing that I was taking inventory away from my best customers, but in retrospect, it turned out to be the correct course of action.

There will come a time in every entrepreneur's life where their loyalty will be challenged by a new opportunity—possibly one he or she has been working toward for a very long time, like getting into Nordstrom was for me. Shorting my loyal customers was a very difficult decision and it will be a hard decision for you when it comes, but you have to draw upon the reasons you went into business in the first place.

The frenzy of Christmas shoppers didn't let up even after the holiday, but there was nothing to ship between Christmas and New Year's, so Conrad and I met to finalize the order entries, total the sales, and close the books on 1990. From September to December we had shipped just under forty-five thousand pairs of boots. Adding in the sales from the previous January and February, the total for the year was $2.2 million. We both knew we had missed fulfilling orders that could easily have added another million dollars, but at this point, I didn't care. At least Alan and Chuck had now witnessed firsthand the disastrous effect of late financing, and they had vowed to be ahead of the curve the next season.

UGG had survived to fight another day, and hopefully this time, we were all better prepared to help it continue to fight.

Top left: Snow-cave show booth. Middle: Snowboard ad.
Bottom right: Snowboard apparel line.

CHAPTER 12

GRADUATION

Entering the corporate world
1991—Sales $3.6 million

High school graduation and entry into the world marks the end of a long—and to a parent, seemingly endless—process toward self-supporting maturity. But it's also the beginning of a new education and new challenges for the child, and a new supporting role for a parent.

UGG began its new life as UGG Holdings, Inc. Until now, I had been a guy on the street selling UGG brand boots. Now I was about to enter the corporate world.

We at last had the funding in place to ensure timely production of boots. Management was on top of the situation and prepared for the coming sales season: Conrad Mouton had a good grip on the accounting and administrative affairs; Tom McGraw was proving to be an excellent sales administrator; and the warehouse, under Rusty Pennock's direction, was organized and efficient.

You will note that the UGG business underwent several corporate changes. The reason is that when new investors agree to fund a new operation, they want their money to go to work immediately in building value with new initiatives to increase the value of their investment. The last thing they want to do is pay off debts and other obligations of the existing company. They also want to make sure they do not inherit any old legal or financial obligations from the existing business. The cleanest and most widely used method is to incorporate a new company, place their new investment into it, and then buy the valuable assets from the old company, but not take on any of the liabilities. This is usually done via an asset purchase agreement. For example, when UGG America was formed, they bought the assets of UGG Imports, and the Rhodeses and I had to personally deal with the liabilities, in particular, continuing to fight the UGHS lawsuit. When UGG Holdings was formed to take over the assets of UGG International, I continued to be the owner of UGG International and had to pay off the liabilities of that company, including buying out Gordon Jackson and Graeme Goodsir. This method has the advantage of the new company getting a fast start into its new venture.

From the outset, Alan had told me that he was going to set in place controls to make the business run under a tight reporting system, with decisions ultimately made by the board. I wasn't certain about my ability to function in my new role as a director. I was ill equipped for a new life of committees, consultants, consensus, closed doors, hidden agendas, and power plays that seem to be endemic in corporate culture. Under Alan Greenway's guidance, I was forced to reinvent myself and let go of my seat-of-the-pants decision-making style that had served the company for the previous twelve years—from the time I had first contacted Country Leather on an impulse.

This is a very common experience for most entrepreneurs who take on venture capital money to expand the business. Along with the money come controls and new "expert advisors" who don't necessarily understand the root of what made the business successful in the first place. This often creates a clash with the core group of founding members who watch their creative ideas get dumbed down to mediocrity in the name of safety and bottom-line profits. The most classic recent example of this is the firing of Steve Jobs by Apple's board, to the company's temporary detriment.

Since UGG was predominantly a California success, I decided to make the establishment of UGG as a national brand my priority; over the next five years, I would rack up almost two million frequent flyer miles pursuing this goal.

My political naïveté, combined with my blind dedication to building our dominance of the market, allowed me to survive this next phase.

The first two items of business were production and quality control. Tom McGraw and I worked on a sales projection for the year and thought we could sell one hundred thousand pairs of boots, but could our suppliers produce them on schedule? We called a meeting of the board of directors and made a formal proposal to place orders with the various manufacturers with a schedule of delivery dates beginning in August. Alan and Chuck believed that we needed to hire a consultant to educate us about the market for sheepskin boots.

Oh no, I thought. *Here we go. Now that we're corporate, the first step is to hire consultants.* Outvoted, I nonetheless cheerfully went along with the decision. Chuck had an associate, Mike Schall, who was a marketing consultant, so we retained him for $20,000.

During the board meetings, I continually had to fall back on—and still fall back on—sincerely exerting my best effort to get my point of view across. Whenever outvoted—and it was a lot—I would always fall back on being a team player rather than trying to subvert the new initiative. You may not always get your way immediately, but it's almost always better to remain a positive part of the team that can then affect positive change from within, than pitting yourself against your colleagues.

Alan and Chuck also thought that we should hire a consultant on product design to advise us, but on this point I held my ground. I maintained that we had the advantage of a limited number of styles, none of which required redesign. It was far more crucial, I argued, to get all the manufacturers working to the same standards with the same quality skins for the coming season. New patterns would only introduce variables that would put quality at risk. We compromised by agreeing to bring on a designer for the next season.

The last major decision resulting from our first meeting was a request for a personnel flowchart to outline the functions and responsibilities of each employee. This was a valuable exercise because Conrad, Tom, and I needed to analyze each function within accounting, sales, marketing, warehouse, and outside customer support. The entrepreneur in me fought against being put in a box, but in the end, I took the title President and Director at Large with all functions reporting through me to the board.

With Alan's guidance, I began the slow process of the letting go of the day-to-day involvement. When people came to me for detailed answers, I trained myself to say, "Do what you think is best." I had always assumed no one else could handle anything about the business as well as I could. Instead, I came to feel a great sense of liberation in being able to concentrate on the big picture and trust that the details would be looked after.

One piece of Alan's advice was invaluable: "Always put things in writing." This was a chore until the internet really took over, and now emails provide a fast, comprehensive trail of requests, queries, and action (or inaction) in every facet of business. Beyond getting things in writing—through email or other means—always be sure to back up your files. It's easy to think of our computers as holding our documents safe, but backing up whatever you have to a cloud, external hard drive, etc., will make your business even more secure and be sure you have records of that in writing that you need.

• • •

The winter of 1990–1991 was disastrous for the ski industry. Snowfall was light over the entire country and many ski areas were not even able to open. Ski retailers were stuck with most of their winter inventory, including our UGG snowboard apparel. Ski shops had trouble paying their bills, and, as usual, UGG was at the tail end of their priorities. UGG was in and out of the apparel business in one short season.

The Ski Show was the quietest I'd seen it in twelve years, although we enjoyed reasonable preordering. The most positive outcome of the show was our meeting there with Jenny Rymill from Sheepskin Manufacturers of Australia, a company that had been trying to market boots under the brand KAROOS, and who also operated a tannery. Since the show resulted in so few orders for her, she offered us her production capabilities for the upcoming season. We saw this resource as insurance for a supply of raw materials, so we ultimately signed a deal to send the patterns and knives to Jenny along with a test order, and we agreed to help them market KAROOS as a secondary brand.

Within three weeks, Mike Schall, our marketing consultant, presented his report, which revealed that UGG was "a Southern California phenomenon" and we needed to expand into other areas of the country. Alan and Chuck felt much better about this pronouncement, but I remember thinking, *Wow, so much money to tell us what I already knew.*

This was my first realization that quite often a statement that I made would be interpreted as hype and optimism, but if a consultant said the same thing, then it was credible and sensible. It occurred to me that I was going to have to learn a more calculated way to communicate with my fellow board members if I wanted to get my own way through consensus.

This is probably the most difficult issue for entrepreneurs to come to grips with. By nature, they have a gift of vision, which is why they are trying to change the world in the first place. Other team members often have entirely different agendas, from profit or risk issues to production or funding issues and other pressures within the company for which they are liable. If all team members are working toward the same vision, it is a good system of checks and balances. However, a heinous situation occurs when a company has been infiltrated by the person who has one agenda—to get to the top—and they will subvert or kill good initiatives simply because their self-interest overrides the company's. Unfortunately, most entrepreneurs do not pick up on this until they see themselves outmaneuvered. By nature, they are simply not wired to fathom Machiavellian plots that don't serve the big-picture vision. Having learned from many years of witnessing this seemingly inherent facet of business, my advice is to never take your proposal into voting meetings without having a majority of potential voters already on your side.

Mike did have some good suggestions for expanding into a bigger market by using the large sporting-goods chains. Tom McGraw picked up the ball and recruited a sales group run by Joe Sheridan, a consultant out of North Carolina who had a national sales force selling athletic shoe brands to all the major retailers, from Footlocker to large independent chains. I wasn't convinced Sheridan's specialty was a perfect match for us, because I saw sheepskin boots as a lifestyle product rather than athletic footwear, but giving sales pitches to the buyers for the big chains at least turned out to be a quick way to gain wider exposure for the brand.

I was thinking along completely different lines. What was it that made Southern California demand so strong that every kid here wanted a pair? For me, it came back to the fact that UGG was authentically tuned in to the surf market. Few people in Michigan, Chicago, Detroit, or New England read *Surfer* magazine, so they weren't our natural market. So what would be the equivalent of surfing in those areas?

I finally got my answer during a road trip in the northeastern states, riding along with some of Joe Sheridan's salesmen. I asked every retailer, "What do kids here do for sport in the winter?"

"Hockey!" was the unanimous reply. "Ice hockey!"

Why hadn't I thought of that? Kids had to switch from their usual footwear when they laced up their skates, so imagine how good a pair of sheepskin boots would feel when they took the skates off, after an hour on the ice. Also, their moms often had to endure sitting around the rink in freezing temperatures. Think how good fleece-lined boots would feel to them!

I found my way to the office of Doug Johnson, the publisher of a Minnesota publication called *Let's Play Hockey*, a magazine founded by Bob Utecht, the famous announcer for the Minnesota North Stars in the early 1970s. Doug told me there were fifty thousand kids enrolled in skating programs throughout the Northeast. I figured that this was probably more than the number of surfers in Southern California. Add in all the hockey moms, and this looked like a viable market. UGG agreed to run a series of ads in Doug's publication to test the response, and I settled in for what I knew would be a long gestation period, confident that in four or five years, hockey would become a huge market for UGG.

Back in San Diego, things were going nicely. It was a pleasure to be relieved of worrying about all the details. Tom McGraw was in discussions with a new sales rep group called the Peters-Fate Group. Its charismatic leader, Steve Fate, had a disciplined team of five reps who were primarily selling to sporting-goods and ski-market retailers with his lines of Thorlo athletic socks and a thermal underwear line in the ski market. Steve was uncertain about taking on UGG at first, but after doing his due diligence with his retailers, he soon became enthusiastic about the UGG brand. It was difficult for me to hand over a $2-million territory I'd personally built over twelve years, but I knew that the territory was too big for just Tom and me to service by ourselves. We brought Peters-Fate on board.

• • •

Since becoming part of the footwear industry in 1978, I had made some observations about the way strong shifts in a society's concerns translate into apparel trends, spawning billion-dollar markets for shoes, T-shirts, or music.

Back in 1979, my friend Matt Fisher took me to the Navy Exchange in San Diego where he could get a great deal on a new running shoe called Nike. He had read about this small company in Oregon that specialized in running shoes and advertised in specialty magazines for runners. I wasn't as impressed by Nike shoes as Matt was. To me, running was boring, something I associated with endless hours of rugby training.

Within a year or two, the sport of jogging took off—coinciding with a societal shift into healthier lifestyles. All the companies specializing in this market, with Nike in the forefront, were swept along in the momentum, driven in part by their own savvy marketing. A few years into the shift, the market was worth hundreds of millions of dollars. Every weekend, across the country, the streets were filled with joggers in logo-decorated fluorescent shorts and tops.

In the mid-1980s, a small company was importing soft, lightweight shoes made of white kid leather, selling them to dance studios and Jazzercise gatherings across the country. It ran ads in small magazines that catered to this tiny niche. Abruptly, the sport of aerobics came into national awareness, bringing in another societal shift with the growth of fitness clubs. All the companies specializing in this niche, most noticeably Reebok, were swept along in the momentum, and another new market worth hundreds of millions of dollars was spawned, along with the fashion trend of Lycra pants and tank tops sporting stylish logos.

In 1991, another new societal shift appeared when the outdoor market took off. Because of our loyalty to Steve and Jeff in supporting the formative infancy and toddler years of the movement, we had earned prime positioning at the Outdoor Retailer Show.

Near the end of July, as I prepared for the show in Reno, I called David Loechner, the show director, to pay for our booth at the main entrance, next to Nike ACG (All Conditions Gear).

"You're not in the show," he said. "We canceled your booking."

"What? What are you talking about?" I said.

"Hey, I called your office a few weeks ago and was handed off to the new head of marketing. Bill something was his name. He said he'd never heard of the Outdoor Show. He told me to cancel the order." Bill Bailey was a friend from Alan's country club. He had a very successful advertising history, both in radio and as owner of his agency in San Diego that included PSA Airlines (now Southwest) in his client list. Although he was in his seventies and was winding down his business, Alan thought he would be good to advise us on all UGG marketing matters.

At the last minute, David was able to squeeze an eight-foot table into the back of the show for us, where we set out a limited display of UGG products. We had nowhere to put our huge lifestyle posters and other merchandising effects we had developed over the years. Our opportunity to showcase Jim Whittaker's validation of the practicality of UGG in the outdoor market was lost.

Since there were a large number of retailers jumping into this market for the first time, they were buying all of the big brands to outfit their stores. Instead of UGG being perceived as one of the big players in the industry, we were generally overlooked in the ensuing buying frenzy.

In 1991, the outdoor ship sailed, and UGG missed the boat.

But a lot of things were going well. We decided to aim for shipping eighty thousand pairs of boots; the orders and financing were in place for timely deliveries for the fall. The samples we received from all of our man-ufacturers looked good, and I was convinced we would be shipping the best-quality boots ever.

As the storms hit Southern California in September, the phones lit up with customer calls. We had a full inventory in the warehouse, ready to ship, so we confidently took in a flood of orders. Determined not to repeat the debacle of late-appearing orders in previous years, Tom McGraw instituted a daily sales-order report that tracked new sales and deducted them from our known availability.

Conrad Mouton was also becoming swamped with the accounting functions, so he hired a bookkeeper to take over the job of receivables.

The overhead was growing.

Most of our advertising in the past year had been handled by the Kent Dial Agency, but Kent was downsizing his business, and he asked me if we would be interested in hiring his assistant, Kate Mulloy. This was around the time when graphic arts technology was making great leaps from literal cut-ting and pasting into computer-generated layouts with digital typefaces and easily manipulated images. Kate was young and understood the potential of this type of production, and we agreed to bring her on staff. From then on, we were able to produce all our flyers and brochures, newsletters and forms in house.

* * *

I spent October and November on the road with the Midwestern and East Coast reps, helping them give footwear "clinics" for their new customers, describing the benefits and care of sheepskin boots—and getting them to try on the boots without socks. As I moved from one area to the next to meet new sales staff, it became obvious I was answering the same questions day after day.

Yes, you can wear them in the snow.

Yes, they insulate, because the sheepskin breathes and keeps the foot at normal body temperature.

Yes, they are washable if you get mud on them.

No, you don't need socks to keep warm.

I noticed that most stores I visited had small video machines used for product demonstrations, so I made a note to bring the idea of an UGG video to the board when I got back from the road. These visits with new customers were like going back four or five years, to the last time I'd had to explain sheepskin boots to California retailers. California buyers no longer asked such questions.

December shipments were going crazy as usual, but at last we had more than enough product to ship. We had arranged for our suppliers to load up our warehouse in December, so production wouldn't be impacted by the long vacation downtime in Australia. We were beginning to trust that any overage we had at Christmas could be sold as fill-ins during January and February the following year.

It was near the end of January before Conrad had the time to compile the accounts for the season. Sales were $3.6 million. We closed the books on another profitable year, and I was feeling optimistic.

For the first time since UGG gained some traction in the early 1980s, we had experienced a season of smooth sailing. All the elements of a good business were in sync, from sales and manufacturing, to warehouse shipping and administration, and they all came together because of one key element—adequate financing

Top: Brian in retro surf ad. *Bottom*: Expanded product brochure.

CHAPTER 13

COLLEGE

"Do you have to wear those steel spikes on ice?"
1992—Sales $5.8 million

Young adults in the early stages of college can find themselves facing new phi-losophies proffered by dubious professors, and the diverse opportunities offered by an array of campus groups. The daily guidance and support from a sympathetic, experienced parent is morphing into a self-reliance that can make the difference between persevering and throwing in the towel.

For the first time in recent years, we shipped all through January. The weather stayed cold, we had plenty of inventory, and the boots continued to fly off retailers' shelves. Good spirits abounded as we kicked off the first board of directors meeting for the year. When Conrad announced the profit results, we high-fived each other for finally getting both product quality and timely delivery from suppliers under control.

I raised the fact that, although we made a profit, and I doubted we were going to have cash flow to last through the summer. Our salary overhead and cost of consultants was over $35,000 per month. Adding to that the increased cost of samples for all of our reps plus the expanded trade show presence, and I doubted if we would last through July.

"So what's the solution?" Alan asked me.

"We have to sell twice as much next season!" I blurted out.

He calmly said, "That's just profitless prosperity," a phrase I had never heard before.

If a product's profit margin is 20 percent and sales are a million dollars, it would make $200,000. But half a million in sales at a 40 percent margin would make the same $200,000—without the extra cost of purchasing, handling, and collecting on the extra sales. Too many entrepreneurs believe "if I can just get to a million dollars, I will be in the money," but that is rarely the case if the profit margins are not high enough. In my experience with UGG, the larger our sales volume became, the less profitable it became due to the ramped up overhead. If you have a yogurt franchise with completely known monthly overhead costs, you can easily predict that, say, 22 percent profit margin will generate $X net profit for the year because you are doing the same thing every day. But, if your business is new or seasonal, or has fast growth or many other variables, it gets more and more difficult to forecast. Refer back to the "Contribution Margin" sidebar previously mentioned in chapter 3 and consult with an accountant.

"But we can't raise our prices," I objected. "The retailers are already bitching because our boots are so expensive."

Still, I knew Alan was right. Because of our low margins, the more sales we made, the bigger our financial problem became. We asked Conrad to calculate the next season's pricing based on increased margins.

Now, many years and many businesses later, I look back at how long it took me to acknowledge and fix the margin dilemma that I perpetuated for thirteen years.

But would I have built a prosperous business or would UGG have been out of business due to no sales if I had insisted on high margins from the beginning? When introducing a completely new product, you will be faced with the pricing dilemma. It is hard to bring an expensive item to market if its value is unknown to the consumers. Possibly the concept of free samples is a solution to overcome this dilemma. Entrepreneurs need to get validation from enough consumers to create a value that corresponds to the higher price. Often you may have to sell the first few items at a loss to get the ball rolling, with the intent to gradually raise the price as it catches on.

For the previous year, Chuck Kaiser had fought just about every idea I came up with to improve the product or sales program. So when the topic of product development came up, I asked Tom McGraw to take the lead. Tom and I had already decided on a range of new colors, but I knew better than to mention them. When Tom proposed them, however, Ice, Sand, Black, Chocolate, and Forest Green were approved with little debate. But then I suggested that we develop a full line of boots with a cupped sole, and Chuck immediately blasted the concept. The original UGG boot's construction simply had a flat sheet of ethyl vinyl acetate (EVA) glued to the bottom of each boot. While this made for a light and comfortable boot, it was slippery on snow and ice. The cupped sole was made from rubber and the edges were raised three-quarters of an inch to reduce wetness from slushy streets.

"What's wrong with our existing boot?" he demanded. "We can sell millions of these just as they are. Why do we need to invent something new?"

"All we have now is an item," Tom explained. "We need a line to offer to buyers, especially in the East, where there's huge waterproof resistance to our current EVA sole."

"And anyway, it's not new," I chimed in. "We're already doing something similar in the Z-Lander boot for the ski market."

Eventually, Tom and I won the day. We decided to call our existing line the UGG Classic and we called the new cupped-sole boot the UGG Ultra—which finally proved acceptable to the cold weather buyers in the Midwest and the East Coast.

The last major discussion in the board meeting was about distribution. Bill Bailey had convinced Alan that surf, action sports, and ski shops were losing propositions, and that we had to sell to the high-end department stores. While I agreed that department stores were the end game, I tried in vain to explain that there was a process to getting there. I told them about the "elephants and mice" analogy I'd learned from the Montgomery Ward buyer and how long it took us to bring Nordstrom on board. Bill and Alan couldn't understand my point.

The outcome was that we brought Kent Dial on as a marketing manager assigned to get us into department stores. Although adding another position in marketing was building up our overhead, I still welcomed his presence. He got it, and I needed an ally to get any initiatives through.

I couldn't wait to get back on the road to work with the reps and add value to the sales effort. Before I could get on the road, I had one more battle to fight. Bill Bailey had decided that we needed a new logo. He had already retained a graphic artist to prepare six new offerings that bore absolutely no resemblance to our existing logo. Nonetheless, I thought the discussion was timely, as I had been considering making a change for some time. The ram's head was becoming problematic in printing, especially in small sizes such as on the heel labels.

Logo designs are so subjective that they almost always flare up into an emotional issue. We all get attached to our pet choices. I loved the existing logo, while Bill favored a design that looked to me like a spider's web.

I was adamant that we keep the words original and Australia and everyone agreed. The typestyle for the letters UGG, however, became a cause of dissension. I explained that we had invested hundreds of thousands of dollars in advertising bearing the existing logo. To preserve what we'd earned, it was important to retain the letters intact, especially the signature style of the middle G larger than the other two letters. That logic prevailed, and we selected the larger G design. This might seem to be a trivial issue, but to me it was one of the most important decisions in UGG's history. The new logo, refined even more now, has worldwide recognition and taken on an almost iconic significance in the market.

I've seen many books devoted to logo design. While it is nice to design the best logo you can, the far bigger issue is how you change or update a logo that has had millions of impressions in the marketplace over several years. I recall when Federal Express changed their logo to FedEx. They retained the exact same typestyle, but equally important, they retained the purple and orange colors, which was their "trade dress," keeping continuity of the recognition of their brand. ("Trade dress" is that subliminal typestyle and coloring that is obvious even when the words can't be read. Other examples of obvious trade dress are Pepsi, Coca-Cola, Toys"R"Us, and Home Depot.)

I had planned to work with our reps in New York a week later, so I asked Chuck to join me there. First, I flew up to Freeport, Maine, to visit L.L. Bean, and I stayed overnight across the street from the buying office. The next morning, a crystal-clear winter day with the air temperature around ten degrees, I walked over for the meeting. They had been successful with the prior season's sell-through and decided to make a big buy—on the condition that we could do a special dark sand color to match items they were buying from other vendors.

"No problem," I told them, knowing I had seen an exact color match in Canterbury's samples from the Bowron tannery.

Elated, I crossed back over the street to a gas station and made a call back to Alan from the public phone box. "Great news, Alan," I said. "We just got an order for four thousand pairs provided we do a special color—"

"What?" Alan interrupted. "We've only just settled on the colors for next season, and you're already going outside our parameters? Go back and tell them they have to take our Sand!"

I stood in the snow, watching clouds of condensation with my every exhalation, shaking my head in disbelief and thinking, He doesn't have a clue. *He doesn't know how hard it was to bring this customer to fruition.* I decided not to go back across the street and throw away the sale. I thought I could win this battle in the months to come.

I met Chuck Kaiser in New York and took him to meetings with Macy's, Saks Fifth Avenue, and Bloomingdales. They all shut us out, explaining that, although they had heard UGG was doing well in California, no one locally was familiar with UGG, and anyway, "We have mud and slush in the winter." Even Danny Wasserman at Tip Top Shoes, the biggest independent shoe store in the area, thought that sheepskin meant slippers. He was already happy with his slipper supply from Acorn.

Mission accomplished! Chuck now saw firsthand that we needed to get the mice running around to get the attention of these big department-store elephants. I believed he knew enough now to relax his resistance to my getting the specialty stores on board first.

I flew down to Atlanta to work with Joe Sheridan's reps at the Super Show, the largest show for the athletic and sporting-goods industry, where we had great success bringing on Sport Mart, Foot Locker, and a host of independent stores.

I then flew to Vegas for the Western Shoe Show. What a change! Kent had designed a beautiful new booth featuring polished wood display walls that mimicked high-end retail shelves, and we commanded a twenty-by-twenty space on the main aisle. Wave after wave of Nordstrom buyers from various regions came by. I felt that, for the first time, UGG and sheepskin comprised a viable category in mainstream retail.

The Peters-Fate reps were in their element when Jamie Walker, the buyer for Sports Chalet, came by and said, "I've set aside a half-million-dollar open-to-buy [budget] for UGG brand boots. You fill out the sizes, colors, and styles, and get back to me."

Other retailers that wrote orders included Meldisco, Kinney Shoes, Genesco, Champs, Track 'n Trail, and Road Runner Sports. The "elephants and mice" phenomenon that the Montgomery Wards buyer had told me about many years ago was becoming evident; we were beginning to go main-stream via the specialty route. On cloud nine, I called Alan to give him the good news.

"Chuck is accusing you of screwing up the Price Club deal," Alan cut in. "We got a ton of back charges and returns that Chuck says you should have negotiated when you did the deal."

"What about the $200,000 in extra cash flow that deal generated from dead inventory?" I asked.

This exchange characterized the extreme highs and lows I was beginning to have to endure. What a tremendous waste of mental effort. In giving up 51 percent control of UGG, I thought I was doing the right thing to assure that the brand survived and thrived. Now we had the financing that had always held up progress, but it came at the cost of egos driving office poli-tics, which began to poison the spirit of the company at a time when UGG needed to be strong and upright.

• • •

In March of 1991, we finally signed the documents to buy 51 percent of a longtime annoyance: the Original American UGHS Company. The current owner, Peter Raffin, had just come off a poor season and was out of cash, looking for a way to keep his factory in Portland, Oregon, alive. We had been through the factory previously and had developed a good relationship with Marlene Howard, the marketing manager for UGHS. Her current sales push was aimed at podiatrists, citing the health benefits of sheepskin in improving blood circulation. They had several good accounts, including Eddie Bauer and the women's department at Nordstrom. But American UGHS were not strong in the general market we dominated. Acquiring the Portland production facility was almost a drawback; I never wanted to be in manufacturing. Cleaning up the brand confusion was paramount to my vision.

We decided to take the UGHS brand out of the market and provide the Oregon factory with patterns and knives to manufacture styles for UGG.

What a delicious moment this was for me personally as I remembered ten years ago when my patent attorney said, "Just beat her in the marketplace."

• • •

Tom McGraw; our graphic artist, Kate Mulloy; and I met to discuss the upcoming action sports and ski trade show schedule where, by now, UGG was dominant in our category in those markets. We also decided to make use of Jim Whittaker's endorsement at the outdoor shows after his successful Mount Everest "Peace Climb." Kate and I also discussed our need for a product demonstration video that could be used for clinics in the retail outlets. She immediately began work on a script.

By the end of May, the orders were pouring in. Under Tom's direction, our sales reps were doing an outstanding job of following up the stragglers, and it looked like we could double the sales of the previous year despite our price increase, which didn't seem to be affecting buying decisions. Now on full-time, Conrad Mouton was an old hand at preparing the purchase orders for our production teams in Australia and New Zealand. They had all been paid on time the previous season, and they had the security of letters of credit for the current year.

In July, chasing an idea we'd had about college football team merchandising, I was in Chicago. While the idea didn't pan out, the sales calls I made while in the city paid off handsomely, and I began to get a good reception and small orders from Chicago-based retailers such as Marshall Fields, J. C. Penney, Chernin's Shoes, and several local Nordstrom stores. I had a great visit with Rob Bondurant, the buyer for Active Endeavors in Evanston. Rob really got the product and its compatibility with the Chicago market, and he placed a good order. I also used this trip to visit all of the hockey rinks in the area to make the rink buyers aware of the product. I wrote orders at every hockey shop and ski shop I visited.

The Chicago market was clearly out of its infancy and growing up fast. The early adopters (consumers who risked buying what might become a high-fashion item and thus be first out of the gate with the latest) had discovered UGG and everyone else would now follow.

But morale back in San Diego was at low ebb. Sales manager Tom McGraw and customer support manager Joel Anderson complained about how Bill Bailey's influence with Alan was disrupting their marketing initiatives. They felt they had to spend too much time proving that Bill's ideas wouldn't work in our market. In addition, Chuck was constantly coming up with new ideas, which confused them about who was really in charge.

When I spoke with Alan, adding my concern to theirs, I was promptly shot as the messenger. Regret that I'd given up 51 percent of the company again surfaced.

No wonder I felt happier and more productive on the road. Working with customers was a very positive experience, even if it entailed solving their problems. I could also keep phone contact with the key people in the office, especially Conrad who had his finger on the pulse of operational matters.

We continued to have success at the Western Shoe Associates Show in August and action sports in September. I flew to Portland to visit the former UGHS factory and shot images for our clinic video. Then I was off to Chicago. We finally displayed product at Hanig's Footwear, a successful chain that had high-visibility stores on Michigan Avenue. Peter Hanig was a seasoned "shoe dog"—the name for someone who has had a long and successful career in the shoe industry—and cracking into his Chicago stores was like breaking into Nordstrom in California. It seemed to me that the highest profile shoe stores are very risk averse, and brands have to show their staying power to warrant inclusion with their other established brands.

• • •

I received a phone call at the end of June from Jim Whittaker, the mountaineer. He said, "My nephew Peter is leading a climb up Mount Kilimanjaro in September. Do you want to come?"

"Do you have to wear those steel spikes on the ice?"

"No, you just walk up," Jim said, making it sound like a lap around the block.

"Okay, sign me up!"

I'd always been a sea-level sportsman. I'd never had an interest in climbing or even hiking, so when I learned that Kilimanjaro is 19,341 feet high, I knew I needed to get into shape. I spent the summer running up the highest hill in Encinitas near my house, to the dizzying height of two hundred feet.

Arriving in Nairobi, Kenya, I met up with my team (fifteen of us) and distributed a pair of boots to everyone before we boarded an old DC-3 to fly into Tanzania, then drive from there to the base of the mountain. That night I had some amazing mental clarity. Maybe it was the air or maybe it was because I was so removed from the responsibilities of day-to-day living, but I pulled out a yellow legal pad and filled two pages with a list of all the paid jobs I'd had in my life so far, in exact chronological order. I wondered if this broad experience might have been a factor in my evolution toward entrepreneurship.

Jim's nephew Peter and wife, Erica, owners of Rainier Mountaineering, had made several expeditions up Kilimanjaro. On this trip, Peter led us the long way around the back of the mountain (the Machame route) to get us acclimatized.

The first four days were a breeze. I left camp in the morning. I had a light backpack carrying water and a sandwich. After a half hour, the porters overtook us at a run, carrying tents, our luggage, five-gallon water drums, and fifty pounds of potatoes and other food, all on their heads. We arrived around noon at a camp where the porters were waiting with a hot lunch ready. After we set off in the afternoon, they ran by us again, carrying everything. When we wearily trudged into camp in the evening, our tents were made up and a hot dinner was waiting.

The porters were amazing athletes, and it was exhausting just to imagine them making this climb day after day. For those of us unaccustomed to walking up mountains, changing into our super-comfy boots became the evening ritual.

The fifth day was not as easy as previous days. We climbed to our last camp at about seventeen thousand feet, where oxygen seemed nonexistent and all vegetation had disappeared. My limbs ached with every step as we toiled up the rocks. We focused on our breathing, since any exertion left us winded and sent blood pounding in our temples, a painful boom boom boom that took forever to return to normal. We ate, then crashed into our sleeping bags in the freezing cold, knowing we would be awakened at 2 AM for the final push to the top.

The final ascent was a blur. After we entered the snow in single file, when the left boot in front of me disappeared, I put my left boot down in the empty footprint. Same with the right boot, and we moved forward this way until just before dawn, when we reached a shelf below a cave where we could stop for hot tea. Although I was semi-delirious, the spectacular scene is still imprinted on my brain. We seemed to be looking down on the entire earth. The horizon was deep red and gold, contrasting with the blacks and purples of the ranges of hills that ran out to eternity. As the first brilliant yellow rays of the sun burst over the horizon, I swear I could see the curvature of the earth below us.

We finally trudged onto the summit around ten in the morning and I unrolled the UGG banner I had brought along. Jim and I held it between us and posed for one of my favorite photographs.

I'd done it. I'd climbed Mount Kilimanjaro. I was done, both physically and emotionally, and I couldn't wait to get out of there!

At last, the group turned for home and we walked across the summit to the downward trail. Two thousand feet below was the Kibo Hut, our next stop, and I looked with dismay at the switchback trail that endlessly crisscrossed the slope.

Halfway across the first switchback, something got ahold of me. I don't know if it was lack of oxygen or just desperation to be off the mountain and elation to be going down, but I stepped off the trail onto the rock scree, and it started sliding underneath my feet. There was no way I was going to spend another two hours walking down the mountain, so I began to run with the tumble of rocks. One of the porters watched with a look of alarm as I plunged by, and he jumped after me. Soon his mouth split into a huge, white-toothed grin as we matched long, slow-motion strides, sliding side by side with the avalanche of loose stones, slowing only enough to jump over each switchback of the trail. With each step, I felt more oxygen in the air, and with more oxygen I got more energy. The euphoria had me taking longer and longer strides, with the spill of loose rocks adding more and more downward momentum. I think I was in the hut in twenty minutes and got in two hours of sleep before the others came in for lunch.

That afternoon, we walked down the gentle trail that most climbers use to come up. What a pleasure to see the vegetation, the monkeys and other wildlife, and finally to sleep comfortably.

Despite never having been on my bucket list, a climb up Mount Kilimanjaro was definitely the experience of a lifetime. But once was sufficient for me. I'm the kind of sportsman who enjoys going down mountains, not ascending them. The highest I ever plan to go is to the top of a fast snowboard run, in a chairlift, with a snowboard on my left boot.

During planning, Peter had suggested we bring items of clothing for the families of the Sherpas. I pulled together about twenty T-shirts that my girls had outgrown, mostly featuring Disney characters. In the ceremony after the climb, all the items (including climbing gear, hiking boots, down jackets, sleeping bags, and so forth) were laid out in piles and the Sherpas were allowed to pick their pile in order of seniority. The kids were running around yelling to their dads which pile they wanted. They were so happy to just get one T-shirt, and to my amazement, none of them had ever heard of Donald Duck or Mickey Mouse or the Little Mermaid. The most desirable pile had about ten writing pads and a box of colored pencils, but the chief Sherpa took them for the school, since they didn't have colored pencils in the village. In retrospect, this experience became the most valuable of the whole Kilimanjaro adventure. When business and California living start to get the better of me, it is great to remember how happy life can be with almost no possessions, and it reminds me that true happiness comes from inside. The knowledge of and connection with my spirit always gives me peace despite any outward circumstance.

• • •

After I got back, I was happy to hear I wasn't needed in the California warehouse this year, since Rusty Pennock, our warehouse manager, had hired a new crew to unpack, sort, and ship the top-quality boots that were being airfreighted to us weekly. Conrad Mouton's staff in the accounting office had increased to handle invoicing and receivables, and Tom McGraw had hired Bob Powell, another customer service rep, to help Joel Anderson coordinate retailer issues. This left me free to travel, so I spent two months on the road visiting our major customers and conducting clinics with new reps.

Our video that Kate Mulloy sent to our best customers made a dramatic difference in the product knowledge of the sales staff at most of the stores I visited. At last I didn't have to answer the same old questions, time after time, since they were visually explained on tape.

Kinney Shoes requested that I visit their Utah and Colorado stores, since this was their first attempt to spread the California success to other states. I was humbled yet elated when greeted in a dozen stores in Salt Lake City and Denver with "Hey, it's Brian Smith—the UGG guy!" Over the next few years, it would be common for many retailers to recognize me as "the UGG guy" from the video.

I went on to Chicago and then farther up the shore of Lake Michigan to Kenosha, Wisconsin. Every fall for years, we had received orders from "Edie from Easy Tan." Whoever she was, Edie had become a substantial mover of UGG product. When I entered her tanning salon, I realized it was an unlikely place to sell boots, but she had a wall full of UGG boxes and a nice display area in front. Edie was an UGG lover, and her passion to share them with others was infectious.

I also visited a nearby shoe store and a sporting goods store in Kenosha, trying to convince them to start with a small order, but neither was interested. *Okay*, I thought. *We'll carry on as if Easy Tan were a true shoe store.*

Dean Brandt, our Minnesota rep, had written orders for Scheels All Sports, so I made a trip to their three stores in Minnesota and North Dakota to provide a product-knowledge clinic to their sales staffs. During our discussions, I learned that winter sportsmen here included ice fishers and hunters who spent hours in blinds, hardly moving, in frigid temperatures. I thought, *Perfect for UGG. I wonder if we should create a marketing campaign just for them?*

• • •

In California, the UGG brand was once again the hot item for Christmas. All the stores were showing large sales increases over the last season. Steve

Fate's entire sales force was out doing the clinics, helping with merchandising, and writing fill-ins for sold-out sizes.

Returning to the office, I found myself entangled in office politics again.

Chuck convinced Alan that we needed to get an outside consultant to review operations and make suggestions, and they had already selected a likely candidate, Ron Cunningham. Ron had recently resigned as VP of finance and administration for the Denver Nuggets, but I would learn later he had also worked for Chuck at his former CPA firm.

For my part, I was happy to have someone independent review the business, so I cooperated with Ron, going over all aspects of the operation, including making a trip to Portland together to review the former UGHS factory. I hoped my participation would deflect some of the heat I was getting from Chuck.

The last creative idea we implemented in 1992 epitomized my adage, "You can't give birth to adults," and it would ultimately affect the destiny of UGG.

When I had been on my road trips, I had developed the habit of scanning magazine racks and checkout displays in local supermarkets to see if *Powder* magazine, *Surfer*, *Surfing*, or *Hockey* were on sale, running our advertisements. I was on a plane coming back home from somewhere when I noticed that the girl sitting next to me was reading *People* magazine. I was fascinated that she spent so much of the flight looking at what the celebrities were wearing.

That magazine is everywhere, I thought. *How do we get mainstream celebrities to wear UGG sheepskin boots?*

In our own small way, we relied on paid celebrity endorsements in our tiny niches of surfing, snowboarding, and hockey, where we could afford it. But Hollywood stars? Alan had once sent a letter to Mel Gibson asking him to consider an endorsement deal us, but we received no reply. I knew a direct approach to a celebrity was out of the question. Also, very few stars will get into endorsing what they wear. Obviously, we didn't have the budget to buy ads in Elle, Shape, Cosmopolitan, or People.

I had been stuck on this celebrity approach problem for a year or more when, one day, I was discussing it during a rare phone conversation with Doug Jensen, my buddy who had helped launch UGG back in 1978.

"Why don't you try stylists?" Doug said.

"Stylists? I've never heard the term. What do they do?"

That's when I found out about the profession inside the celebrity world generically called *stylists*—hair stylists, makeup artists, wardrobe design-ers, and the like—who work closely with celebrities. After a lot of digging, I found and purchased a mailing list of about four hundred Hollywood stylists.

We sent a form letter to every person on the list, offering them a free pair of boots in any UGG style; all they had to do was complete the form and send it back. This experiment in outreach went out before we shut the warehouse down for Christmas, and we waited to see what would happen. Though I had been a bit frustrated to see no movement on this front for some time, I finally realized that the idea had still been gestating, and it was only now that we had finally given birth to our celebrity marketing plan. None of us knew how long its infancy would be, but I was happy to know it was finally moving forward.

Top: Mount Everest Peace climb ad. *Bottom left*: Brian and Jim Whittaker on summit of Kilimanjaro. *Bottom right*: Revised logo.

CHAPTER 14

ON YOUR OWN

Moving along nicely
1993—Sales $9 million

As the first few years of college pass by, new life goals take form and new associations are made based upon common benefits and lifestyles. Dorms provide the freedom of communal living areas where the safety net of close associations provides safety from the big world.

Cold weather continued through January and February of 1993, and shipping of refill orders was brisk. We had been very profitable for the three months going into Christmas 1992, and for the first time since starting the company, I felt no need for outside financing for the coming year. The factories in Australia and New Zealand had been working overtime in December to give us the cushion of inventory we needed before they took their six-week annual vacation.

The fate of the Portland, Oregon, factory was not so clear. Ron made a case to rely solely on subcontract factories. Should we close Portland down or keep it running? The opposing case was that we should continue to use our same suppliers for now (defending our known and existing supply) and keep Portland on line for future growth (to attack new opportunities and broaden our supplier base).

Something my marketing professor at UCLA once said helped me strategize: "You have to defend before you attack."

To have made a wholesale shift away from our suppliers would incur at least a year of new learning curves in quality control as well as disrupting the flow of high quality skins that had taken so long to develop. We agreed to keep our existing suppliers in place and give a series of small orders to the Oregon factory, where we could monitor their efficiency, batch by batch.

At this same board meeting, we presented the new colors for the '94/95 line. In addition to our standard Natural and Sand, we chose Navy, Cinnamon, Green, Chocolate, and a new Black sheepskin treated as shiny Napa leather, which we thought would be attractive to the Midwestern market, where shiny black leather was popular.

For several seasons I had wanted a desert-boot style in our line and had been working toward this with John Chandler, the designer and factory manager at Canterbury Sheepskin in New Zealand. I presented to the board the fruits of John's labor, a modified version of one of Canterbury's shoe designs. We agreed to go ahead with it, naming it Nullabor after the vast desert in the middle of Australia.

Doug Price from Canterbury had sent us a new style of lightweight slip-on shoe he wanted us to consider. Always an advocate of expanding the UGG line so he had more to sell, Tom McGraw loved it immediately. He and I both saw potential in developing a line of fashion shoes for the women's market.

• • •

Our first response from my celebrity marketing mailer at the end of the year before was disappointing; of the four hundred names on our Hollywood stylists list, only forty responded to our offer of free boots. Still, I knew this was a long-term experiment, so we quickly sent the complimentary boots to each of the stylists who replied, and I decided to wait out the next stage of its growth.

We noticed a huge change at ASR, Outdoor Retailer, and Western Shoe Associates trade shows, which all occurred in February. For fourteen years we had set up our booths in the various shows, put on our game faces, and hoped a fair number of buyers dropped in. That year, we had order-writing tables going constantly, and our reps had back-to-back meetings scheduled. The drop-ins had to either wait for a rep or make an appointment to come back.

At the Super Show in Atlanta, activity was much lighter, but for me it was a memorable show in other ways. Bill De Vries, the president of Footlocker and Champs, came into the booth with his entourage of Kinney buyers who were likewise part of the Woolworth footwear conglomerate. He looked over our new line and quickly zeroed in on the Nullabor desert boot.

"I've been watching UGG for several years," he said, "and I see the category of sheepskin footwear becoming a new, viable segment of the market."

Wow! I remembered how nervous I had been walking into surf shops in 1979, and how out of place and insignificant I felt at the first few trade shows. Bill invited me to visit his office in the Woolworth building the next month, and despite the fact that most Americans hadn't yet heard of UGG, I felt we'd made it to the heights of recognition. To top things off, Mark Sullivan, the publisher of *Footwear News*, approached us to do an article on sheepskin products in general and UGG in particular for his magazine.

• • •

In early February, at Chuck Kaiser's instigation, we agreed to bring Ron Cunningham on full-time as CFO, overseeing Conrad Mouton and the Portland, Oregon, factory. Conrad had just come through a blistering year-end frenzy of shipping, inventory control, collections, and accounting, and wanted to take a six-week vacation with his family back to his homeland, South Africa. Halfway into Conrad's time off, Ron announced to Alan, Chuck, and me that he had found a discrepancy of $200,000 in Conrad's bookkeeping. I was on the road almost the entire month and, try as I may, I could get no specific details of the error. There was no open mention of stealing or misappropriation, but when I got back to the office there was a general air that Conrad had to go. I fought vehemently against this; Conrad had been instrumental in saving the company in several bad times. He was as honest as anyone I knew, and I couldn't imagine him embezzling.

But I also realized Alan and Chuck had their minds made up. When Conrad returned, I bounced the idea off him going up to Portland to run the factory. He knew how politically charged the environment had become and was willing to be relocated where he'd be out of the line of fire, and the board voted to make him the factory manager. Within several months, the discrepancy somehow evaporated. The books balanced perfectly.

Upon my return to the office, Alan Greenway told me that Chuck had decided to move from Houston to San Diego and wanted a full-time job with UGG as chief operating officer. My heart sank, and I did my best to persuade Alan not to go along with Chuck's plan.

"Don't rock the boat," Alan told me. "Chuck can be really disruptive, so let's humor him. You just need to act more like a director and we can control him."

• • •

Once again, I looked forward to hitting the road. Dean Brandt, our Midwestern sales rep, had finally arranged a meeting with Dayton's in Minneapolis, one of the largest department store chains in the Midwest, which was just beginning to discover UGG. The buyer said that she was being asked every day if Dayton's carried UGG brand boots. Most of the inquiries were coming from women who wanted to wear them at the hockey rinks.

Aha, I thought. *The hockey infant is crawling and getting around.* Buoyed by this news, I dropped in on Doug Johnson at *Let's Play Hockey*. I relayed what I'd just learned at Dayton's, and we toyed around with ideas on how to amplify the wave. We finally decided to create a "Hockey Mom" ad campaign, which would run weekly in his newspaper. Each week, kids would write in with stories about why their mom should be picked as Hockey Mom of the Week, a pair of sheepskin boots as the prize for winning moms. Doug was also airing a weekly TV show at the time, so we sponsored it with a full-minute advertisement opening each week's show.

In New York, we finally got a significant order from Lord and Taylor department stores. Danny Wasserman at Tip Top Shoes also became a new customer; he admitted he'd been getting a steady stream of customers asking for UGG products.

I had no idea what was driving the interest in the New York, but I decided to begin advertising in the city.

On my way back to San Diego, I got my first order from Hanover Shoes in Pennsylvania and also got a big order from American Eagle Outfitters.

• • •

Chuck Kaiser continued to be a worrisome factor for me. Within months of his full-time presence, I had noticed the first instances of closed-door meetings where he would pull various members of the staff into his office for one-on-one chats. At first I tried to ignore it, but as the months passed I became aware of a shift in the way the staff interacted. We had always been very inclusive in meetings on marketing, sales, and product development, inviting everyone to weigh in on the issues. Now I sensed the staff's reluctance to speak freely, and it was disconcerting.

Quite often it came down to a battle of wills between Chuck and me, with the others waiting to see who came out on top before venturing their own opinion.

This went on for several months. I felt the life force of the company being sapped.

Mental poisons include fear, anger, envy, jealousy, suspicion, and intolerance. If my life isn't going smoothly, I can usually pinpoint the source of the conflict and proactively work on it. I had been sleeping fitfully for months because of my conflict with Chuck, and one night I thought over the list of mental toxins that might be affecting me. Envy and jealousy were not an issue for me, but I had a large dose of the others.

Over the years, I have developed a method of handling those times when I lie in bed, unable to sleep because of the loop that plays over and over in my head. In the universe, the two extremes of emotion are fear and love. Most fears are imaginary, and they seem most real when you are in that half-awake, half-asleep state. When I finally realize that I am in that dread mode, I simply say to myself, "I choose love. I choose love. I choose love," over and over again. In a short period of time, I feel my muscles and temples relax and as soon as that happens, I drift back off to sleep. You do not have to be an entrepreneur or business owner to do this. Fears come to everybody and I urge you to give it a try when you next feel the dread.

After a lot of soul-searching, I decided that my title of president was not as important as the well-being of UGG. Knowing it was impossible for the staff to serve two masters, I decided to relieve the conflict. I resigned as president and agreed to stay on salary as a director.

I felt disconsolate for a few weeks, but finally snapped out of it after asking myself, *What can I do best to grow the company and make UGG a national brand?* I came up with four goals: help Conrad succeed in Portland, promote the brand on the road, get a deal involving the US Olympics team for the Olympics coming up in Norway, and ramp up the celebrity marketing.

Conrad Mouton's activities in Portland had surprised everyone. Instead of feeling sorry for himself for being exiled to a remote outpost, Conrad had requested help from Canterbury Sheepskin. John Chandler, their factory manager, had flown to Portland to advise him on efficiencies. John trained Portland's cutters in how to maximize the yield from skins, taught the sewers techniques to speed up the stitching operation, improved the gluing and sole attachment processes, and provided Conrad with cost-accounting formats to track the profitability of each product in the line.

Conrad proved that he could profitably supply our tall Classic boots five dollars cheaper than our best suppliers in Australia, while matching the best of them in quality.

• • •

Back in March, during the hectic ski industries show, Joe Zahran walked into the booth. Joe was with the Sara Lee Company, which owned the Champion brand of clothing; Champion had been selected as official outfitters of the Olympic Team to go to Lillehammer, Norway, the following February. Since Champion didn't sell footwear, Joe was looking at all the winter footwear at the show to identify candidates for inclusion in the official Olympics athletic gear.

Joe was skeptical of UGG, although he knew many of the Olympic skiers owned sheepskin boots and swore by them. I offered to send him samples if we made the short list of suppliers.

In May, Joe called to let me know that UGG had indeed made the short list and he wanted us to send samples of the Ultra and Nullabor boots to the ski team's representative for testing. Despite Alan's skepticism—"You'll never get in! Our boots aren't fully waterproof."—and Chuck's ability to invent obstacles—"We can't ship samples to the US Olympic team. They're not made in America!"—I went ahead and sent the samples. I asked Joe when he'd need the full supply of boots, in the event we were selected; with Joe's information, Tom, Conrad, and I began to calculate when production would have to start at the Oregon facility.

When I called Joe in July, he told me that the product committee for the USOC had conducted a spirited discussion on footwear selection, and a clear consensus emerged for not selecting UGG. However, the team representative held his ground, saying that a majority of the athletes already owned their sheepskin boots and were demanding that UGG be the boot of choice, and the final vote of the committee was to use UGG products in Lillehammer.

Cathy Menck was my USOC contact. She sent me a swatch of the blue material from the US team's uniforms. Two weeks later I sent Cathy three different shades of blue sheepskin to review for compatibility with the Olympic uniforms. She selected a very deep navy blue with a purple hue, and ordered one pair of boots to be made to judge the full effect. When we received the boots from Canterbury a week later, Cathy took them to the committee and quickly received its go-ahead, provided we could make soles to match. Conrad sent a swatch of sheepskin to the soles supplier, and a week later he had a perfect color match that likewise got the committee's approval. With that out of the way, things moved fast. In July we received Champion's official order for about five hundred pairs of tall Ultra boots and another five hundred pairs of black Nullabor shoes, enough for the committee members, officials, sponsors, and dignitaries as well as the athletes.

One condition of our inclusion as an official supplier was that the boots must be certifiably *Made In America*. Conrad, Tom, and I had already researched this and learned that, even if the skins were from New Zealand, as long as the manufacturing was done in Oregon, we qualified. Conrad had priced a used side-stitching machine, so we bought it immediately to get the stitching crew in practice. This also helped our overall production strategy, because the machine enabled Conrad to bid to supply our Ultra line requirements.

With our production rolling along and the Olympics deal on track, it was time to focus on expanding our brand in the United States. Since we'd firmly established UGG awareness in California and were making headway in Utah and Colorado, I decided to make the Midwest and the East Coast my next targets for evangelizing UGG. Joel Anderson, who had been running our customer service operations, had been getting more involved in helping Tom manage the sales force. Joel had mentioned that he wanted to move back to the Midwest, and since our East Coast territory was becoming pretty active and I was falling behind on my road trips, we offered to help him rent an apartment in Chicago and promoted him to manager of all the sales reps east of the Rockies.

Our preseason orders indicated we were going to exceed the prior year by two million dollars. Ron had implemented a new computer system that simplified invoicing, making inventory control more predictable and finally automating production orders for Australia and New Zealand.

Free from the details of the day-to-day business, I was in entrepreneur heaven. I did still have some daily responsibilities. For example, to all of my loyal customers, I was still the UGG guy, and they turned to me whenever they had problems. Maintaining customer loyalty was typically what kept me in touch with the office.

The fall trade shows revealed a host of new sheepskin brands on display, such as Qwaruba and Aussie Dogs, but they were friendly competitors who carefully avoided using the UGG trademark to describe their look-alike boots.

I was amused during the setup at ASR, when Doug Otto, whose Deckers booth was directly across the aisle, came up to me with a sheepish grin. Doug had started his business in the late 1970s selling surf brands; his current success was TEVA sandals. In recent years, Doug had asked if he could buy us; his sandal business dried up every winter, just as our boot business dried up every summer. Doug was clearly looking for something to sustain his outdoor business during his lean seasons.

On display at his booth were short and tall sheepskin boots; instead of traditional soles, he had attached them to TEVA rubber soles and had the TEVA nylon strapping crisscrossing the uppers with snaps at the ankles. While I was a bit peeved that we had another competitor to deal with, I didn't think his boots would catch on except with die-hard TEVA fans around the campfire.

• • •

No sooner had we begun the shipping in September than store buyers started calling us in a panic, asking why we sold to Price Club. They had UGG boots on sale for only ten dollars over the surf shops' cost, and they couldn't compete with those prices.

We were all stunned. We hadn't allowed the UGG brand into the discount clubs, so we did some detective work and discovered there were about ten Price Club outlets in Southern California with the boots; each seemed to have about two hundred and fifty pairs in stock. This meant we should look for the culprit among our customers who had purchased about twenty-five hundred pairs, a large order that would be easy to spot.

During the Ski Show the previous March, a buying group came to us claiming to have a large sporting-goods distribution network in Europe. They had ordered a container of boots, roughly twenty-two hundred pairs. At the time, we had thought it strange that they'd wanted the boots shipped via Los Angeles, when they had claimed their office was in Switzerland, but they had explained that they needed to check the product before sending it to Europe. Now, this was circumstantial evidence that they were the source selling our products to discount outlets.

Luckily, UGG boots were such a hot item that the clubs sold out in a week or so, and the episode didn't really affect our regular retailers during the rest of the season. But it had been a close thing, so from then on we had a new mantra for the salespeople: "If an order looks too good to be true, it probably is."

That season, we also noticed many of our competitors were displaying products at the autumn shows copied from the samples and colors we had displayed at our March shows. This was a pattern we'd come to accept as an inevitable downside of our leadership in the market. We began work on a new line to be debuted the following February, refining the bulky toe shape, considering roll-tops and side-cuts, and improving the heel shapes.

Meanwhile, we received fresh orders for the Lillehammer Winter Olympics: sixty-five pairs for the CBS sports crew, seventy-five pairs for the Coke-sponsored on-air commentators, and a unique pair for NBC's anchorman Bryant Gumbel. The blue-dyed skins had arrived at Conrad's factory from Bowrons, and he was on track with production. He surprised us with the news that his costing for the Ultra style was coming in at eight dollars cheaper than we were buying from Australian sources. Once banished from the company's head office in disgrace, accused of a bogus $200,000 shortfall in the accounts, Conrad had become a star performer as head of operations in Oregon.

Because Champion Footwear was formally the one and only outfitter of the US Olympic Team, we learned that we were forbidden by our contract with them from any publicity that might identify UGG as an "official supplier" to the US Olympic Team. This was disconcerting. What good is it supplying the Olympic team if we're not allowed to tell anyone about it?

I huddled with Tom McGraw and Kate Mulloy, and we sent out a press release craftily worded: "UGG has been selected by Champion, the Official Outfitters of the US Olympic Team . . ." Immediately, we were approached by the *L.A. Times*, *Footwear News*, and *Women's Wear Daily*, who all published great articles highlighting the UGG brand.

• • •

My last project for 1993 began when Alan called on short notice to tell me that Bill Bailey had made an appointment to meet an old associate of his at the Rancho Santa Fe Inn, and Alan wanted me to go along with him.

Earlier in the year, Bill had declared: "Radio is the future for UGG!" We had managed to keep most of his brainstorms in check, but this time he had Alan's and Chuck's ears. Bill wanted to launch radio campaigns in all the major metropolitan markets. Apparently, he had a contact in the media who could get us discount rates for a big buy.

Tom McGraw, Joel Anderson, and I had a heck of a time trying to explain to Bill that UGG was a tactile buy: customers had to touch and feel the boots—or at least see them!—and, most important, try them on. We pointed out that very few people in the radio markets he was proposing had ever heard of UGG, but he argued this was exactly why he wanted to run the ads.

Fortunately, our anti-radio-advertising faction carried the day on the logic that the money could be used more effectively to enhance sales in our existing stores, provide free products for salesmen's prizes, and expand comprehensive clinics in the retail stores. With that, we had assumed Bill's idea was laid to rest.

Six months later, however, I found out his associate in the radio business who had planted the advertising idea was Ed McLaughlin, who had begun his career around the same time as Bill, in the late 1950s. McLaughlin had gone on to become President of ABC Radio Networks, headquartered in New York. Then in 1987, he'd launched his own group called EFM Networks, devoted to talk radio. McLaughlin soon added *The Rush Limbaugh Show*. By 1990, the show had become a fixture on more than two hundred radio stations.

My vision for building UGG as a fashionable, comfortable footwear brand with appeal for every American was now under serious threat. From a marketing standpoint, entangling UGG brand's carefully groomed image with a particular political movement was madness. I had previously observed that Alan had a penchant for being associated with high-profile celebrities, and it became clear to me the lure of Rush Limbaugh, the right's emerging pied-piper, was a force I might not be able to overcome.

Top: Let's Play Hockey ad. *Middle*: Lillehammer Olympic photo. Bottom left: Teva sheepskin boot. *Bottom right*: Nullabor desert boot

CHAPTER 15

FINAL EXAMS

Why didn't they teach me this in business courses?
1994—$11 million

As we get ready for the final exams, armed and prepared with the knowledge we've soaked up, we look to the future with hope and enthusiasm for what comes next, knowing that it's both new territory we anticipate and yet also something that we cannot fully prepare for.

I didn't see much of my family for the first two months of 1994. On January 1, I left to tour all the manufacturers in Australia and New Zealand to discuss allocations for the following season. Since we estimated we could sell 220,000 pairs, we made allocations based on past loyalty, quality, capacity, and reliability. The Portland factory, Canterbury, Jackson group, and a new supplier, Cromptons, comprised our sourcing. They had all been paid the previous season, and we had financing in place to get them started on time. It all seemed so easy compared with those endless years when financing was in doubt.

I was still relishing my position as director at large, not reporting directly to Ron, and I looked forward to traveling to Australia and to Norway as spokesperson for UGG. It was during the two weeks between trips that Kate came up to me in the office with the new brochure for next season.

The downside of not reporting to Ron was that I was cut out of many of the projects that I had loved. One of them was creating the brochures each season, and I knew that no one could do them as well as me. However, as I began to turn the pages and assess the photography, the layout, the typestyles, the flow of products from boots to slippers to kids, the introduction of the new Avenue line, and finally the sandals, I said to Kate, "This is fabulous!" Even the color and texture of the paper was perfect. I knew at that moment I could not have done such a good job myself.

I was finally free of all of the details of day-to-day operations. The first time I felt tasks being taken from me by Chuck and Ron, it was like having my fingernails pulled out. Now I wondered why I had fought it so much. Alan had kept exhorting me to "act more like a director," and now I finally understood where he had been leading me.

The most common mind-set all entrepreneurs share comes from thinking, No one can do it as well as I. *You have to just let go, delegate, and resign yourself to the fact that the outcome will not be perfect. Quite often, you will be pleasantly surprised.*

• • •

Though some things were going well, others were hitting unexpected walls. "You can't represent UGG with your Australian accent," argued Chuck. "We need to be represented by Americans." Chuck had been a naysayer all along, but now that the Olympic deal was coming to fruition, he wanted to be in the limelight. But I held my ground.

"I've negotiated this whole deal with Champion. No one there has ever complained that I have an Australian accent," I told him.

"Well, you're not going as our sole representative. Tom will have to go with you."

I welcomed this. I had deliberately spent a lot of time out of the office to avoid the power plays, leaving Tom to deal with things, so we had become somewhat estranged. Here was a chance to reconnect with him. Eager to be at the center of the sports world, Tom and I headed to Norway and the Olympics.

Since the boots had been sent to Champion a month earlier, there wasn't anything urgent for us to attend to. Tom and I made our way to our hotel in the Olympic Village where all the dignitaries from Sara Lee, Champion's owner, were staying. The hotel consisted of three stories of stacked, prefabricated wooden boxes, each ten feet by twenty feet, with two cots and a small basin and heater. The toilets were at the end of the hall. All this luxury cost only $1,400 per night!

The evening we arrived, I was approached by the US team doctor.

He told that when they decided to use sheepskin boots for the team, he didn't think they would work. But when the boots had arrived just the day before, he'd taken a pair and stood out in the parking lot from 2 AM to 4 AM—with no socks. Even though it was about minus twenty degrees, he had been amazed that his feet had never changed temperature. "Those boots are amazing!" he exclaimed.

Over the next two days, Tom and I fitted boots for every athlete on the team, except Tonya Harding and Nancy Kerrigan, who were under tight security. After everyone had been fitted, Tom and I were free to roam the town and be tourists. We attended the opening ceremony, and a few of the events.

After a day and night in Oslo, Tom and I left for home, proud of UGG, thrilled to have been part of the Olympics, and our friendship intact.

• • •

After only two days at home, I left for the Ski and Shoe Shows. The sell-through at retail had been exceptionally strong the previous winter, and it showed in the size of the orders that were being written at the shows. Again, Jamie Walker from Sports Chalet told our reps, "I want seven thousand pairs for our first delivery, so make out the sizes, styles, and colors, and bring me the paperwork to sign off."

For the first time since 1979, I didn't take a single order myself. Instead, I took on the role of greeter and facilitator with longtime customers. New inquiries I handed off to the reps. Ahhh, the luxury of walking into the shows to see that Kent Dial had the booth already set up with the product and graphics looking fabulous.

Every entrepreneur knows the hardest business development chore is to plan for, pack, deliver, unpack, and set up a tradeshow booth. With envy, they all notice the bigger companies that can afford to hire crews to do this, and then they watch the owner walk in on opening day and hang out with the sales crew. I estimate that I set up over seventy tradeshows before I reached this dream.

By the time we finished the Super Show, the Action Sports, and Outdoor shows, Tom McGraw and I were confident we would set another sales record, this time approaching twelve million dollars for the season. After a trip to New York, where I met with Andy Knause from Kinneys—who requested a sample of every style and every color—I knew this would be a banner year.

• • •

Six weeks later, Alan called. "This is very serious," he informed me. "Chuck has called an emergency meeting tomorrow. He's accusing you of defrauding the company."

"What are you talking about?" I asked. "What's he up to now?"

"It's to do with expense reimbursements. You'd better do your homework and come prepared with answers."

Once again, I had to drop the project I was working on and devote precious time to fending off another of Chuck's offensives. I met with Alan,

Chuck, and Peter Raffin at a hotel that Alan owned, and the tension in the room was obvious the moment I walked through the door.

Chuck started in on me immediately. "You're a cheat, untrustworthy . . ." and on and on he went.

"What are you talking about?" I calmly asked him.

"You've been double dipping your expense reimbursements. Look, here," he said, pulling out some receipts.

I quickly laid out my credit card statements and showed them all that Chuck's accusation was entirely unfounded, which was followed by a stunned silence.

"What the *#!%& are you playing at?" I raged at them. "Can't you see this is what Chuck always does? Why the hell can't he get in the boat and row with the rest of us, instead of sitting off to the side and firing torpedoes at us all the time? Can't you see how low the morale of the office has fallen because of this backstabbing? I've had it with Chuck's closed-door meetings. I never want to see another closed door in our offices again!"

As a result of all this, Chuck was rarely seen in the San Diego office from then on. Ron Cunningham, who I think was pleased with this development, slid in to take over control of all operations.

> *Anyone who has been an employee of a large organization can probably relate to a confined and stifling atmosphere. Of all the aspects in managing employees (or being an employee) the most insidious is dealing with people who distort or hide the truth, ignore the truth, offer half-truths, etc., in an effort to manipulate their way into more power. When the milk bottle stops shaking, cream rises.*

• • •

Two major marketing initiatives consumed me for the rest of the year. One set UGG off on a positive trajectory, while the other had a more debatable outcome.

First, at the footwear industries show that Chuck and I attended in Boca Raton, one of the speakers was Carol Cone, the principal of Cone Communications. At that time, Carol was pitching cause marketing, mutually beneficial tie-ins between for-profit businesses and social or charitable non-profit organizations. Carol was convinced that public relations was far more effective than advertising at getting a product noticed. Chuck was impressed with her enthusiasm and invited Carol to come to San Diego to give her sales pitch to the UGG board. It went over well, and the board voted to use her services to create a message for the brand that, as spokesperson, I would take on a PR circuit. The concept intrigued me and I put all my efforts into making it a success. I loved the travel, and being the evangelist for UGG was natural for me.

In August, I went to the Cone headquarters in Boston, where we spent several days developing the UGG message. We decided to ignore the rugged surf and outdoor attributes and instead promote UGG as "comfort casual." I loved the concept; it would relate to both men and women and wasn't geographically restrictive, unlike surfing and skiing imagery. We set to work preparing a press kit and handouts for all the PR contacts in the Cone database. Linda Goldstein scheduled my visits to cities, venues, and media outlets, and she was assigned to accompany me to all of the interviews. After the message was refined, we spent two days in mock interviews.

I spent the next month practicing my pitch, then returned to Boston in mid-October to begin the road show. We attended morning radio drive shows, various Boston magazine interviews, local television event interviews, and *AdWeek* magazine.

All of the fashion editors published articles about the new comfort-casual UGG line, and I began to realize the power of volunteered third-party endorsements to bolster the credibility of our claims, rather than relying on the questionable effectiveness of ad buys.

Then we repeated the same types of events in Minneapolis and Chicago.

The response we met on the media tour proved to me that PR is worth more than conventional advertising we could afford.

Although the concept of public relations remains unchanged to this day, the method of distributing information is reinventing itself seemingly daily. What used to be a laborious task of physically mailing flyers to prospective interviewers at specific magazines or radio and TV shows, a much bigger viewing audience can be contacted directly through Facebook, LinkedIn, Twitter, personal blogs, and YouTube. If you haven't availed yourself of these new tools, I recommend you select and begin working with one of the many social media training companies that have proliferated over the past few years.

• • •

The second initiative: In June, Alan announced, "We should advertise on *The Rush Limbaugh Show.*"

Immediately the office was polarized. The sales and marketing departments were solidly against the idea, but Chuck and Alan had irreversibly bought into Bill Bailey's contention that "radio is the future." More worrisome for me was Alan's penchant for wanting to be associated with famous personalities, a characteristic I first noticed when Alan had negotiated to bring Greg Norman into his golf venture. I had no problem with Alan's delight in hanging out with celebrities, but I had a huge problem with how much money he was prepared to pay for the privilege.

"Rush Limbaugh is the antithesis of the casual-comfort image we're trying to establish," I argued. "The guy is all suits and starched shirts. He has no fashion credibility to bring to UGG."

We held a long meeting that included the marketing staff, Steve Fate representing the California sales force, and several important customers. To be honest, the room was split on the issue. The sales force and some customers were of the opinion that any publicity is good publicity, knowing that a surge in exposure from Rush's show would be good for sales. I tried to argue that this was very short-sighted; we'd gained a lot of momentum with the new image we were building, and if we lost it, it would take years to rebuild.

Ultimately, we decided to commission a study by the Peter Harris Market Research Group before we made a final decision. The Harris team was instructed to do a national survey to identify the most credible spokespeople for UGG and to specifically ask about Rush Limbaugh's potential effect on the buying public.

A month later, Bill Bailey wrote a summary of the findings, which concluded that Paul Hogan ("Crocodile Dundee") would be the best spokesperson for UGG, and Paul Harvey (another radio talk show host) also fit the UGG demographic and would ruffle no feathers. According to the survey, although Rush Limbaugh could greatly extend awareness of the brand, if we associated with him, we could expect a boycott of the UGG brand and also a loss of retailers. Increased exposure through Limbaugh could result in additional sales from a half to a million pairs, yet UGG would run the risk of alienating up to 34 percent of its customer base.

Thank God, I thought. *There is no way this can go forward with such mixed findings.* We agreed to hold a board meeting to decide the direction of the Rush Limbaugh initiative.

I spent the weekend honing my presentation for the board, specifically aimed at educating them on the essence of the UGG brand and how far we had come in creating a lifestyle image. My aim was to be convincing on the essential point that we should stay our course on marketing a fashionable, comfortable image, while continuing our efforts to gain celebrity adoption. I also set up a spreadsheet that calculated the total cost of one-minute spots, five times a week, for three months, at nearly $500,000—for radio! This was more than the cost of running full-page ads in *Glamour* and *ELLE* magazines for an entire season.

On Monday morning, prior to the meeting, I walked into the office adjacent to the boardroom to find Alan and Chuck, airline tickets in hand, comparing their flight arrangements to New York. On the desk were front-row tickets to the taping of a live Rush Limbaugh TV show scheduled for the following week.

What the hell? I thought, feeling my chest tighten.

Alan and Chuck hurriedly put away the papers and returned with me to the boardroom. Bill Bailey presented his report, outlining that Paul Harvey would be the best person to advertise with, based on the Harris Group research, but that Rush Limbaugh would also increase UGG sales. I did my best to prevail with my irrefutable logic, but felt like I was trying to explain rainbows to a blind man. Alan, Chuck, and Bill were deaf to any facts that might change their minds. The vote was simply a show of conforming to boardroom protocol.

Years later, I was reading Tom Clancy's *Op-Center,* when I came across the following paragraph that stopped me:

"Paul Hood had been in enough politically and emotionally charged situations, both in Government and on Wall Street, to know that the outcome of important meetings was often decided before the meetings were called. Key people, often no more than two, spoke or got together beforehand. By the time everyone else arrived, the talk was mostly for show."

It seems obvious in retrospect, but I had no clue that this kind of situation was so endemic that it would be offhandedly mentioned in a work of fiction. Why didn't they teach this stuff in business school?

I had been outvoted, and the Rush Limbaugh advertising buy was approved. I had to think about the big picture, to put my wounded ego aside, and since I'd given it my best shot and lost, now was the time to exercise ingenuity in making the best of the situation.

> *Learn to let go. I've found that the disappointments hardest to bear are those which never come, as was the case with the Limbaugh initiative.*

Letters were sent and phone calls placed to our best customers announcing the campaign. Their reaction was mixed. Those customers who loved Rush were ecstatic, while others were shocked. Kinney's loved the idea. Nordstrom buyers . . . not so much.

I insisted that if Rush Limbaugh was going to pitch UGG on the air, then I was going to give him the same clinic our sales reps got beforehand. I went to New York in early September. First I met with Mark Sullivan at Footwear News to discuss an article and to alert him to the advertising we'd be doing with Rush. Mark told me the magazine's editors had decided to run with UGG sandals on the cover of the next issue.

I eventually met Rush in his office near Times Square in New York City. His advertising salesman had told me I had a half hour with Rush at the most, so I immediately pulled out the pair of boots in Rush's size I had brought with me, and asked him to try them on.

He really didn't want to try them on, claiming he hated hot feet and he could sell them regardless.

I knew that he was already missing a critical point: Your feet don't get hot in sheepskin boots. So I held my ground and insisted Rush take off just one shoe and sock to try them. He was still resistant, so I bluffed. I told him flat out, "If you don't try on the boot, we're not going to go ahead with the program."

He grudgingly took off a shoe and sock and pulled on one boot. Naturally, there was the universal "Oh my God!" reaction. Limbaugh kept the boot on for the remainder of my allotted half hour as I went through all the selling points and the literature I had brought. Finally, as I was packing up to leave, I asked him if his foot was hot.

"No!" he exclaimed in surprise. "It's the same temperature as my other foot. I could tell the audience about this . . . and this . . . and that," he continued, going through the sales points in the brochures. As I left his office, I felt comfortable he would do a capable job of pitching the attributes of the UGG product to his audience now that he was a believer.

Excitement was high as we sat around our desks in mid-September waiting for the clock to hit 9 AM. Rush was going to introduce UGG to his audience for the first time. He began his show with, "Hi, folks. Tomorrow we're going to have a new sponsor, UGG brand sheepskin boots." Within sixty seconds, our switchboard was overwhelmed with calls, effectively shutting it down for order taking—a situation that made it impossible for existing retailers to reorder—and didn't recover until after Christmas.

Most of the calls were from stockbrokers aware of Rush's impact on Snapple sales in previous years. They all wanted to know, "Are you guys publicly traded? Can we buy stock in UGG? Are you going public soon?"

From all across the country, our reps reported in with stories of customers walking into retailers and saying, "Rush told us to buy UGG boots. What do they look like?" My favorite story was of an elderly grandmother who went into Spyder Surf, a hardcore store in Hermosa Beach, telling the clerks, "I saw the UGG sign out front, and Rush said I have to get them." She bought six pairs for her family.

Another anomaly was the number of truck stop stores that called us wanting to carry the line. Apparently, huge numbers of truckers listen to the *Rush Limbaugh Show* while they're driving. We never shipped to the truck stops; it wasn't the market we were hoping for.

For our regular customers, we finally found the solution to the phone-order bottleneck by having them fax in their orders. Soon, even our fax lines couldn't handle the volume.

Tom McGraw and I knew we were going to miss out on a lot of fill-in sales for the season, while from the product-logistics side, we were doing everything right. Containers of boots left the manufacturers on time in June, and our warehouse had incoming stock turned around for delivery to retailers quickly. But as December drew to a close, we still had a lot of inventory on hand that we could have shipped to our regular customers—if they'd been able to get through to us at the height of the season.

Our marketing team estimated we could have sold at least another million dollars of boots over the previous year's total, even if we hadn't done the Rush Limbaugh ad campaign. Financially the campaign lost us a lot of sales, but I rationalized they were positively offset by the millions of American listeners who now knew the word UGG and would recognize the brand in the seasons to come.

·   ·   ·

My last trip for the season was to visit Nick Whitworth in Cornwall, England. We had a potential distributor in London who wanted to handle UGG products for the UK, but we didn't own the trademark there. Nick, an enterprising young manufacturer, had registered the trademark for the UK and had a factory in a little surfing town in Cornwall. After two pleasant days discussing how we could buy his trademark registration from him, we finally agreed on a deal, and I returned to the office to hand off the final negotiations to Ron Cunningham.

Sales for the season came in at just over eleven million dollars, just one million short of our goal. Nonetheless, we had come through a frustrating challenge—and passed the test.

New warehouse before and after.

CHAPTER 16

ADULTHOOD

Out to Discover the World
1995—Sales $11 million

It's time for the matured young adult to strike out for a new career and make a life. Options are weighed and alternatives scrutinized. Choices made now will decide the future. Will they join a dynamic team and change the world or strike out on their own to do it their way? The world is their oyster.

January 1995 was a month of intense soul-searching. I had always envisioned millions of Americans wearing UGG boots, with "casual comfort" at the core of the brand's identity. Although my partners had a common goal in sales, they differed on marketing strategy, and for that and other reasons, I wasn't happy with my work environment.

Our celebrity marketing efforts were beginning to take hold. Every month, UGG brand boots were showing up in more and more TV programs, movies, and magazine spreads, yet I could get no support from the board to advertise to this market. Our financial situation worried me above all else. We had just come off a very profitable season, yet our buying *The Rush Limbaugh Show* airtime, which sucked over half a million dollars out of our cash flow without generating any real improvement in sales, filled me with dread. I kept waking in the middle of the night with a sense of foreboding I couldn't put my finger on. I felt a sense of déjà vu. All through the eighties, I had been the victim (and perpetrator) of too much spending of our seasons' income on advertising, samples, and trade shows, which crippled my ability to finance production for the coming season. That was why I had to bring Alan and Chuck on board in the first place. They had not learned from painful experience as I had, and they were about to repeat the same mistakes I'd made.

It was when Alan walked in on the first day of February and announced that Rush was great and he wanted to sign a three-month contract with him to sell our newly created sandal line for the spring that I made up my mind. *This is suicide*, I told myself. *This will bankrupt the company, and all the hard work will have been for nothing. We have to find a buyer!*

Two days later, at the Atlanta Airport on my way to the Super Show, I saw Doug Otto from Deckers Outdoor Corporation waiting in baggage claim.

Goose bumps formed on my arms. I felt them tingle down my back.

Oh my God, I thought. *It's perfect!*

Doug burst into a big smile when he saw me and we greeted each other warmly.

"Doug," I said, "if we're ever going to do this deal, now is the time."

"Are you for real?" he asked. "When can we start?"

As soon as I was settled into the UGG booth and the show got underway, I called Alan and received his support to begin negotiations. We instructed Ron Cunningham to begin the due-diligence discussions. Alan went along with my one, absolute condition: Chuck Kaiser would not be allowed to talk with anyone at Deckers.

I knew that Deckers was a good fit. Their cash flow was the opposite of ours: they were always cash strapped in the winter, since they shipped summer products. The UGG brand was a perfect counterbalance, since the same customer service people could be kept busy year-round, and the warehouse staff could operate for twelve months simply by swapping out products. Also, since both TEVA and UGG were footwear brands, they could be serviced by the same reps and be shown at the same trade shows. Ron Cunningham and Deckers' CFO, Diana Wilson, spent the month of February discussing the logistics of a merger.

In the meantime, we had tremendous success at the Western Shoe Association show in Las Vegas. Most of our buyers doubled their orders from the previous year; Kinney started with 25–30,000 pairs, and J. C. Penney wanted the UGG line for its West Coast stores. The problem of the ordering frustrations from our Rush Limbaugh adventure seemed to have subsided because the inventory they received had good sell-through. The Ski Show was equally vibrant. It was surprising to me how many customers there remarked approvingly on the Rush campaign, and since these buyers were very brand and image conscious, my overall fear of brand damage was minimized.

• • •

Early in March, the UGG and Decker teams met at the San Diego Yacht Club to discuss the sale of the company. Doug Otto and Diana Wilson represented Deckers; Alan Greenway, Ron Cunningham, and I were there for UGG. Various possible scenarios were tossed around: an infusion of Deckers' capital into UGG, a merger of the companies for a stock swap, licensing the UGG brand.

We arrived at an outright sale of UGG Holdings, Inc., to Deckers Outdoor Corp. Now all we had to do was establish a price. We finally landed on a selling price for UGG comprising cash, plus a royalty on future sales. Diana wanted a firm commitment that we would not shop our deal to other potential buyers, and, in a stroke of genius, Alan asked for a loan from Deckers to guarantee its sole participation. Through that one simple request, we had shored up our ability to get product for the next season.

One of Doug's conditions was that I be brought back on as director of marketing to facilitate the transition to the Deckers marketing team. Another Deckers condition was that they did not want to have anything to do with our Portland factory.

We all shook hands, and the deal was done. Ron and Diana were tasked with finalizing the last details and liaising with the attorneys.

• • •

Because of the success of our public relations tour the previous season, we decided to do another one, focused on a national newspaper. Linda Goldstein from Cone Communications had arranged the tour in the Chicago area. Our final appointment was with Elizabeth Snead, the fashion editor at *USA Today*. Elizabeth had double-booked our appointment time, so she gave us five minutes before she had to leave for another meeting. Realizing I would not be able to follow our usual lengthy script, I just pulled out the folder I carried with photos of celebrities in sheepskin boots and started flipping pages. Neil Young, flip. Tom Petty, flip. Sting, flip. Patrick Swayze, flip. Brooke Shields, flip.

The next photo was from the cover of London tabloid *The Daily Mail*, showing Pamela Anderson on the set of Baywatch, standing around in her red lifeguard swimsuit and tall, natural sheepskin boots. This wasn't the "casual comfort" image I wanted to portray to a national audience, so I quickly flipped past the Pamela Anderson photo to a lifestyle shot of Heather Locklear for *InStyle* magazine.

"Wait a second. Back up," Elizabeth said. "Who's that?"

Before I knew it, she had written down the photographer's name, made a copy of the Pam Anderson photo, and grabbed one of our press release folders. Then, she was gone to her meeting. Linda and I walked out, feeling like we had blown it.

At the airport next morning, waiting for my flight back to California, I bought a copy of *USA Today* and did my usual scan of the articles. When

I turned to the Lifestyle section, my jaw dropped. Front and center on the first page was the photo of Pam Anderson in her tall, natural boots, above a brief but lively story on the new direction of footwear fashions. When I got back to San Diego, the office was buzzing. The phones rang all day from consumers wanting to know who carried UGG in their area and from retailers asking how they could buy UGG boots for their stores. I did not see this red swimsuit image as how the product was worn, but it did prove that celebrity sells. I'm sure that photo generated millions more imprints than any other photo I had in the presentation I had prepared for Elizabeth.

Some would call it luck, but to this day, I simply accept these moments as being when the universe kicks in and overrides my own limiting beliefs.

• • •

My mission remained to build the brand, and I continued to stay on the road, working with the reps while Ron Cunningham handled the transition with Diana Wilson from Deckers. Ron and I had been offered positions with Deckers, and all of the UGG staff in San Diego were told they would be welcome to stay on board as long as they were willing to relocate to Santa Barbara; none did.

Finishing up the road trip in Boston, I mulled over my future. Did I want to move my family to Santa Barbara? Did I want to be a full-time salaried employee in a public company, with shareholders and analysts looking at every penny of expense? How could I best utilize my talents as an entrepreneur to build the UGG brand?

I called Alan and met to seek his advice.

"Brian," he began, "you don't have a political bone in your body. Deckers is a public company and will have rigid internal controls and a defined hierarchy. You won't survive six months inside an organization like that, with a defined job description. Your greatest strength is thinking outside the box, but that quality is viewed with risk in big companies. If every idea you come up with has to go through a formal committee approval process, you'll suffocate. Just remember how little support you got for your hockey program. You're the classic entrepreneur, never tied down by protocols. My advice is that you avoid a salaried position and see if you can negotiate a consulting contract."

And so, a week before the scheduled closure, I drove to Santa Barbara, met with Doug Otto, and told him I would stay on as a consultant, based in San Diego, for two years. My mission would be to help with product development and work with the Deckers' sales reps on the road, to familiarize them with the product.

I would not be living my longtime dream of owning and running a huge international company; however, I felt fortunate to have held together a business with such promise and release it to blossom with someone else's guidance.

Each and every one of us should work to be successful and happy,
but having given it our best shot, we must sit back and enjoy both
what we have and what we've created, no matter how it turns out.

• • •

On August 1, we signed the deal and the sale was complete.

For the rest of the year, Deckers kept the San Diego office intact and we continued to handle the shipping and marketing. The staff was incentivized to stay on until Christmas, but the attrition grew as our personnel found new jobs.

I spent some time in Portland helping Conrad wind down the operation there. He had proven to be adept at factory management and was providing sixty thousand pairs for the season. I tried my best to convince Deckers to keep production at full pace, since history had shown that the in-season reorders accounted for 25 percent on top of preseason orders, but Deckers had other plans. I guessed that since they were publicly traded, they were under scrutiny by Wall Street and would rather forego three million dollars in sales than get caught with unsold inventory at year's end.

Every two weeks, Deckers held a steering committee meeting at Doug's second home in Mussel Shoals on the Pacific coast, a few miles south of their corporate office. Ron Cunningham and I were participants. At each meeting, Ron made his case that the San Diego office should be left intact to do the shipping, and I spoke against it. To me, one of the most important benefits in orchestrating the sale was to merge the shipping operations to keep year-round productivity.

Ultimately, the vote was made to close down San Diego and move the entire unshipped product into Deckers' TEVA warehouse.

I had expected that, once we finalized the sale of UGG, I would have no more dealings with Chuck Kaiser. Unfortunately, there was one final thrust still to parry.

He told me he wanted me to join with him in a lawsuit against Alan, believing that he could have negotiated a better outcome from the sale but was prevented from doing so. I couldn't believe Chuck was turning to me to help him. I knew Alan had loaned him the $100,000 to get into the business in the first place, and now Chuck had millions in the bank as a result. I ignored him.

At the time, I thought of Chuck as one of the worst people I'd even met, but I have come to realize that the most antagonistic people that I have encountered along the way have profoundly advanced my understanding of business and life.

Now, after seventeen years of starting (some successful, some not), running, and selling new businesses, I have mellowed on label-ing the participants as "good guys" or "bad guys." In retrospect, everyone involved in the building of UGG—from suppliers, service providers, and customers, to staff, investors, and myself—was sim-ply doing what they thought was best for their own success. Holding on to anger does no one any good. As they say, resentment is like swallowing poison and waiting for the other person to die.

Adversity is a crucial element of spiritual growth, and so instead of resenting those instances that hurt so badly at the time, I cherish them.

The simple act of acknowledging and releasing my former adversaries has allowed me freedom and great peace of mind.

• • •

The TEVA sales manager, Ron Page, announced he would not keep any of the UGG sales reps; he intended to hand the line over exclusively to the TEVA sales force. I tried in vain to influence his decision enough to retain our best performers but only succeeded in convincing him to bring on one of the young Deckers employees, Devin Byrnes, to handle the UGG brand's Southern California dealers.

Later, when the national sales meeting for TEVA reps was held at the Four Seasons hotel in Santa Barbara, Ron Page invited me to speak at the assembly for their official introduction to the UGG brand. At the time, TEVA sales were around five times the sales of the UGG brand.

"Congratulations," I began my address to about one hundred and fifty sales people, "you have just inherited a fabulous brand. I believe the potential of UGG is $200 million."

I felt a low groan ripple out across the audience, and I was a bit embarrassed. The room seemed to be saying, "Who the hell does this guy think he's kidding?"

Not even I could have foreseen that, sixteen years later, the UGG brand would be a worldwide fashion phenomenon generating sales exceeding $1 billion annually. One of the reasons that Deckers eventually achieved this staggering achievement had to do with the last piece of luck that occurred under our watch.

For several years, Trudie Styler—actor, activist, and wife of the musician Sting—would call the office each Christmas and order around twenty pairs of boots to send to her friends and family in the UK. This year she called with an urgent request.

"Oh my God," she said. "I've just been to a seminar that changed my life! I want you to find the absolute best pair of the tall, sand-color boots and here's where to send them."

We took down the details: send to Oprah Winfrey at *The Oprah Winfrey Show* in Chicago. The new marketing team, led by UGG president Connie Rishwain, forged an alliance with the Oprah team over the next few years, with UGG appearing for the first time on "Oprah's Favorite Things" five years later in 2000.

•   •   •

Over the years, it's become apparent that I am a darned good business starter—much more so than a business operator. I'm the first to admit that taking UGG from fifteen million dollars to one billion in sales required a completely different skill set than I possess. My passion now is to speak to business students and would-be entrepreneurs, to consult and to mentor those who have passion and ideas, yet do not know how to progress. I love sharing my powerful concept: "You can't give birth to adults." My years of ineffective capital raising, which crippled potential sales, made me realize that entrepreneurs desperately need to learn this skill. I have developed a coaching program to help early stage business owners structure and design an effective presentation deck, and to create the best script and delivery pitch when in front of potential investors.

The story of Deckers taking UGG and refining it into a truly international brand of class and sophistication is deserving of its own book. For almost twenty years now, I have marveled at the ability of UGG president Connie Rishwain to translate her New York shoe fashion knowledge into the comfort arena and build a formidable team of manufacturers, administrators, marketers, a sales force, and even company-owned retail stores.

While keeping the surfer heritage of the early brand intact, she has steered UGG through Oprah's love affair on her TV shows, advertising in strategic fashion magazines, masterful product placement, and building UGG into an iconic brand far bigger than the sheepskin boots at its core.

• • •

I had conceived and given birth to UGG, watched over its infancy, enjoyed its spirited youth, and hung on for dear life through its unpredictable teen-age phases. Now it was time for me to let it go as an adult and let it make a life for itself within Deckers.

I thought back to those times in my early twenties when I was an audi-tor at the AMP Society in Sydney when I handled a check for twenty-two million dollars. As huge as it seemed at the time, it now looked tiny com-pared with the potential I saw for the UGG business going forward.

Laura and I had millions in the bank. We bought a new minivan and had new carpet laid throughout the house. That's all we wanted. Whenever we discussed it, we just looked at each other and laughed, realizing we must have been living like millionaires all along!

I've been asked many times: "What was the best part of building UGG?" Here's my answer:

No matter where I travel in the world, every time I see the UGG logo on the back of someone's boots on the street, my heart does a little skip and dance. I feel so proud to have started something that has given that luxurious touch to millions of feet. The livelihood that UGG has brought to the many hundreds of faithful retailers who have become my friends and the relationships I enjoyed with such a diverse array of manufacturers, tanneries, sales reps, and staff is, looking back, the true fulfillment of an entrepreneur's dream.

Acknowledgments

Thanks to my Publicist, Simon Warwick-Smith for your persistent reminders to begin writing. To friends Jon Shafqat, Stan Cobbold, Vincent Gordon, and Stuart Graham for reading the first draft and encouraging me to continue.

To Karen Misuraca, Dennis Mathis, Gretchen Stelter, and Henry Covey, who brought their amazing editing skills to tighten my story into a fast, easily readable memoir/business book.

To Suzie Baziuk, Maynard Kartvedt, Lawrence Kahn, Kathleen and Jim Felt, Lorraine Pedrick-Allen, and Greg and Allyn Reid for providing input on the last drafts.

And to my many friends, associates and acquaintances who have shown great interest and encouragement in bringing the book to you, I am deeply indebted.

Accelerate Your Path to Freedom and Happiness

Go to www.BrianSmithSpeaker.com for
***Free* Tools to Help You Start and Grow Your New Business**

One Year of Free (2-Minute) Videos

Receive one of Brian's "Boots-on-the-Ground" business tips every Friday.

Five-Part Video Series: "How to Discover and Start Your Own Business"

Discover your passion and best options, with beginners steps to get started and how to grow the business of your dreams.

Free E-Book: *The Boomapreneur Revolution*

It's estimated that there are thirty-four million "Boomapreneurs" in the United States, people over fifty who want to start their own businesses. Society paints them as "over the hill" and unemployable, but in fact they're intelligent, healthy, active, wiser, and have vast amounts of energy and capital to contribute to improving their own lifestyles and the economy at large.

Join this growing wave of fifty- and sixty-year olds who are still thirty and forty in their minds. Go to www.boomapreneur.com to download your FREE e-book. You are also invited to submit your own story of how you built your business as a boomapreneur for inclusion in our upcoming hard copy of *The Boomapreneur Revolution.*

Keynote Speaking

Visit www.BrianSmithSpeaker.com to book an inspirational and motivating keynote speech at your next meeting.